The Sign Language of Faith

Property of :

GARY MARK WAYNE KEITH

Gerd Theissen

The Sign Language of Faith

Opportunities for Preaching Today

SCM PRESS LTD

Translated by John Bowden from the German
Zeichensprache des Glaubens. Chancen der Predigt heute,
published 1994 by Christian Kaiser Verlag/Gütersloher
Verlagshaus, Gütersloh.

0 334 02598 2

First British edition published 1995
by SCM Press Ltd,
26–30 Tottenham Road, London N1 4BZ

Typeset at The Spartan Press Ltd,
Lymington, Hants
and printed in Great Britain by
Mackays of Chatham, Kent

To the Theological Faculty of the University of Neuchâtel
in gratitude for their award of an honorary doctorate

Contents

Preface

This book is a brief homiletics, written by someone who is not a specialist in that area. It began from an invitation to give a lecture on the relationship between exegesis and homiletics within a further education programme of the theological faculties of the Suisse Romande. The single lecture that had been planned grew into four, which were delivered in Fribourg on 1 and 2 March 1993. In them I attempted to give an account of what I am doing when I preach, what I intend and what is out of my hands. In other words, I attempted to become aware of the homiletics implicit in my own preaching. The only literature on homiletics that I used in preparing the lectures was the excellent anthology edited by F.Wintzer, *Predigt* (1989), and with much benefit the relevant sections in the handbooks of practical theology edited by G.Otto and D.Rössler. I learned a great deal from the discussions in Fribourg. For that I am grateful to all those who took part, the doctoral students and pastors of the 'troisième cycle théologique pratique', especially my colleagues M.Douze (Fribourg), P.L.Dubied (Neuchâtel), H.Mottu (Geneva) and B.Reymond (Lausanne). Their criticisms and further reflections helped me to put my own experience of preaching in a wider current of experience and reflection. The revised lectures appeared in French, published by Labor et Fides.[1]

The German edition is a revised version of these lectures, to which a new second chapter has been added on basic questions of exegesis in relation to homiletics. The other chapters have been revised and provided with notes, which refer above all to specialist literature on homiletics. What I have learned from reading R.Bohren, K.F.Daiber, H.W.Dannowski, A.Denecke, W.Engemann, O.Fuchs, A.Grözinger, M.Josuttis, K.Meyer zu Uptrup, E.Lange, G.Otto and D.Rössler – to mention just a few – is often not expressed adequately in the notes. The notes do not indicate all the times I thought 'Aha' when reading, browsing in or leafing through the pages. I did not want to write a homiletics in which I treated all the problems systematically or described the whole of the present state of reflection on the science of preaching.

My main concern was to show that preaching has far greater opportunities than it is often accorded today. I feel depressed when I find pastors who attach little value to their sermons. I respect the experiences which have led to such resignation, but I cannot accept the conclusions, especially as my experiences have been different. In writing I had in view the many theologians whom I am training. I would very much like to motivate them towards preaching – above all for the sake of their congregations. Congregations can sense whether or not preachers are motivated, whether they prepare sermons lovingly or with inner reluctance. And I am also concerned about the preachers themselves. The time and place where Protestant theologians prepare their sermons is the centre of their 'spirituality'. Here is an opportunity for them to develop their own theology and work on their own Christian identity. If it is true that one has to go through a phase of irritation, disquiet, defeat or depression before many sermons, it is also true that here theologians can find a source of motivation for all their actions. The experience that despite the experiences of alienation from biblical and religious traditions a spark keeps springing from the text into our lives can become the inner support of a theological existence.

One objection, however, must be taken seriously. As a rule I preach at university services. I can organize my work in such a way that I have quiet times to prepare for these sermons. The setting of my experience of preaching is different from that of a normal congregation. So the question arises whether the ideas of preaching developed here can be transferred to and realized in another context. I also recognize that academic literature on homiletics has the same problem, since as a rule it arises in an academic milieu, remote from what goes on in the local church. I would like to make three points on this issue.

First, I sent the first version of the book to younger pastors known to me who preach under 'normal conditions'. I am particularly grateful to Petra von Gemünden, Andreas Feldtkeller, Gudrun Ortwein and Helmut Schwier for their critical responses. Of course I was especially pleased when I was told that it had proved possible for some of my suggestions actually to be tried out in sermons.

Secondly, an appendix to the book contains five sermons, only one of which was given at a university service. Four of them come from Petra von Gemünden. They were written for churches in Munich and Coburg – in 'normal' circumstances. They were not written for publication, but they are the kind of sermons which I had in mind when I wrote this book. I am grateful to Petra von Gemünden for allowing me to reproduce them here.

Finally, I have taken note of the results of empirical research into preaching. I have no intention of summing up these results. But it was important for me to check my own experience by them.

The title of the book may sound unusual for a work on homiletics. I am aware that 'the sign language of faith' covers more than preaching. It includes liturgy and sacraments, church architecture and church music, books and pictures. However, in the Protestant tradition the sermon is the centre of the symbolic language of Christian faith. This book puts forward the view that the Bible is the basis of a sign language which even today gives people the opportunity of entering into dialogue with an ultimate reality. Preaching has the task of bringing new life to this sign language in order to make this opportunity a real one. Among all the opportunities for preaching, this is the decisive one. Nothing has changed here since preaching began.

The origin of this book is closely connected with the Suisse Romande. Therefore I am dedicating it to the theological faculty of the University of Neuchâtel, which awarded me an honorary doctorate in 1989.

Finally, a word of thanks to all those who helped in the preparation of this book: to Manfred Weber of Christian Kaiser/Gütersloher Verlagshaus, who supported the project from the beginning; Annette Merz, who read through the manuscript critically; Helga Wolf and Wega Schmidt-Thomée for preparing different drafts of the manuscript; and above all those who responded to my sermons critically, first and foremost among them a very critical listener, my wife.

Heidelberg, Easter 1994
Gerd Theissen

Introduction: Dimensions of Preaching

Any preaching interprets the biblical tradition for the present. Here exegesis and homiletics work together. Exegesis defines the meaning which the biblical text once had at the time of its origin. Homiletics seeks to contribute to transforming this past meaning into motivation for present-day experience and behaviour through preaching. Here exegesis and preaching seem to have almost opposite tasks: exegesis arrives at its results in a strictly 'historical-critical' way, regardless of whether these results are beneficial or harmful, usable or unusable in the present. But preaching aims at speaking to the men and women of its time and giving them guidelines for their lives. It is not interested in anything that was significant only in the past. If one looks at the relationship between exegesis and preaching only in this way, one arrives at a contrast between past and present, exegesis and application, historical meaning and significance for the present.

Nevertheless, there is a continuity between exegesis and preaching. Exegesis shows that each text is already itself the result of a process of tradition. Factors of tradition are at work in every text: sources, pre-existing ideas, images and words. The author has reorganized them and made them speak to the audience of the day. To this degree any sermon continues what has already been begun in the text: in any sermon, texts which come from the past are re-actualized for the present. Now if exegesis arrives at a fundamentally new understanding of the historical process of tradition in the Bible, this has consequences for the understanding of preaching. For the way in which texts in the Bible are actualized is a model for the way in which the Bible is actualized in the present. The relationship between the biblical authors and their traditions is a model for the relationship between a preacher in the present and the text of the Bible.

Now in fact over the last twenty-five years a new understanding of processes of tradition in the Bible has been worked out.[1] Tradition has been described as a generative process. The repetition of the text in the process of tradition is in reality a re-creation. This is especially true of oral tradition. The tradents have internalized the most important structures of the genres, narratives and images in the texts, so that they are capable of 'creating' these texts anew on the basis of the structures which they contain.

In a simplified way, the old and the new understandings of the process of tradition can be contrasted as follows. According to the accepted understanding, authors take over traditions from the past. They modify these traditions in respect of their own situation by omissions, additions, changes – in short, by redaction. From these alterations it is possible to infer the 'intention' of the author. The author has been understood by the audience if they have grasped this intention – which includes an 'introduction' to the author; for an 'intention' is always an inner reality. So we find three stages which follow one another in time:

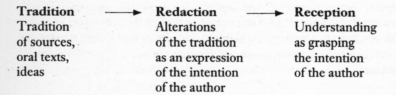

Tradition ⟶	**Redaction** ⟶	**Reception**
Tradition of sources, oral texts, ideas	Alterations of the tradition as an expression of the intention of the author	Understanding as grasping the intention of the author

By contrast, the new image of the process of tradition emphasizes that tradition, redaction and reception are equally products of a common text-world inhabited by tradents, redactors and recipients.[2] Their world is recorded in the structures of the text-world. This is a kind of 'langue' (with grammatical rules and different elements), to which tradition, redaction and reception are related as different 'paroles'. The process of tradition succeeds where tradents and redactors share a common world of meanings, forms and motives. Similarly, understanding is successful where all speak a common 'language', i.e. participate in a collective sign system, can control its rules and include its elements. So our scheme has to be changed as follows:

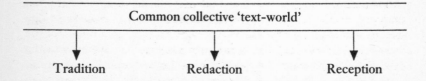

Common collective 'text-world'

Tradition   Redaction   Reception

Whereas tradition, redaction and reception follow one another in time (they have a diachronic relationship), the collective world of the text which underlies them is contemporaneous with all the stages: it is 'synchronous' with the phases of tradition, redaction and reception. It 'generates' the different phases of the process of tradition.[3]

This new model of the process of tradition has been further developed by intertextuality studies.[4]According to these, what is called 'tradition' in the model described above can be dissolved into many pre-texts (in principle, an unlimited number), all of which resonate with the origin of the text (the redaction). Often their resonance is unclear, so that it is described as 'intertextual noise'. But even as such 'noise' which is only perceived as a background, it is present at the reading of the text. Intertextuality studies have made us sensitive to the fact that the relationship of a text to its pre-texts can assume very different forms: from explicit quotation through allusion to merely the implicit presence of a pre-text in the text. Intertextuality studies to some degree turn diffuse 'noise' into articulated resonance. Here three major groups of intertextual references can be distinguished.

1. Intended and marked intertextuality
This appears when an author (or tradent) deliberately refers to a previous pre-text in his text and makes this reference explicitly clear. The clearest form of intended and marked intertextuality is quotation with an express formula to indicate that it is a quotation. The author marks the text referred to in this way (referentiality), shares this reference with the reader (communicativity), and characterizes the status of the pre-text in the formula indicating the quotation, for example by mentioning 'holy scripture' (auto-reflectivity). Other forms of marking can take the place of the quotation formula, for example commentary on a statement which emphasizes that this statement is an already existing pre-text.

2. However, there can also be intended intertexuality where the reference to the pre-text (or pre-texts) is not explicitly marked. In that case the reader and hearer (if they are familiar with the text-world) can discover the reference to pre-texts in corresponding patterns in the texts, in fields of images, words and motifs (structurality as a mark of intertextuality). Or particularly pregnant elements are selected from

pre-texts (selectivity). Finally, the way in which the pre-text is dealt with (ironic allusion, authoritative solemnity, alienation, etc.) can make clear that the text has inter-textual references. The text enters into a dialogue with the pre-text. Thus 'dialogicity' is a further characteristic of intertextuality.

3. In addition to this, in all texts there is unintended intertextuality which is not marked, in so far as they participate in a common text-world. All the texts in this text-world also as it were 'make a noise' if the one text is understood.

The phenomenon of intertextuality is nothing new in biblical exegesis. Any reader of the Bible will soon note how many references to the 'Old Testament' there are in the New Testament, and how varied these references are: from explicit quotation, through allusions, to texts in 'Old Testament' language, from the proof of prophecy through typology and allegory to timeless authoritative quotation. In addition, exegesis has discovered many intertextual relationships between the individual writings: common genres, traditions, topics, fields and traditions of images, word-fields, formulae and so on. This variety of intertextual relationships is important for preaching, because preaching is con-stituted by biblical intertextuality – by reference to an individual text (in preaching on a text) and to parts of the 'overall system of texts' (when preaching on a theme). Now if within the Bible there is already a variety of references of texts to their pre-texts, preaching, too, may experiment with a greater variety of relations to the text.

If we extend the model of the process of tradition presented above yet again, by indicating the great variety of intertextual relationships, we arrive at the following picture:

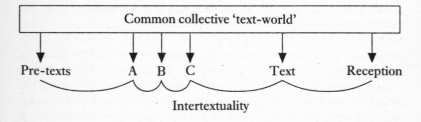

But even this model is still too simple. Is it the case that the collective 'text-world' from which the individual texts are produced stands in a timeless way above the various pre-texts and the sequence of text and reception? No! The collective text-world is also historical. At the level of the text-world there are long-term changes, and at the level of concrete texts there are short-term changes. The biblical text-world is different from the world of meanings in which modern men and women live. One could now say that it is precisely here that we have the decisive difference between the processes of tradition in the Bible and the tradition of the Bible in the modern world. At that time everything moved in one and the same world of meaning; today we must engage in a process of transference, and first reconstruct the past biblical text-world in order to make understanding possible. But that would be a mistake: within the process of biblical tradition, new text-worlds often struggled laboriously against old ones. Monotheism displaced earlier forms of religion in the Old Testament. In earliest Christianity the Christian message was communicated to Gentiles who did not share essential presuppositions of understanding (like monotheism). So even at that time the common text-world could not always be presupposed, and often first had to be 'constructed'. This common text-world (regardless of whether it was presupposed or first had to be constructed) underlies both the transition from tradition to redaction and the transition from redaction to reception.

Anyone who handed on a miracle story in earliest Christianity of course repeated the story that he had once heard. But if he was a good story-teller, he knew the structural pattern of miracle stories, the typical motifs and themes. So in every 'repetition' of the old miracle story he created a new story on the basis of this knowledge – with slight changes which in his eyes were not changes at all. For they were based on an existing collective treasury of motifs and themes. Here tradition and redaction are on each occasion new creations on the basis of the same collective store of possibilities. In contrast to the usual image of the process of tradition, changes in the existing tradition were measured not only by the 'original' but by the virtual store of all text possibilities. Every concrete motif in a miracle story is always a selection from other possible motifs. Handing down and editing means participating in a shared text-world.

An example may help to make this idea clear. On the basis of my familiarity with the motifs and structural patterns of earliest Christian miracle stories, I shall tell a new one. This new story is composed of ten Markan miracle stories:[5]

5.1 They came to the other side of the sea, to the country of the Gerasenes. 7.24 And he entered a house and would not have anyone know it; yet he could not be hid. 7.32 And they brought to him a man who was deaf. 2.4 And when they could not get near him because of the crowd, they removed the roof above him; and when they had made an opening, they let him down. 10.47 And he began to cry out and say, 'Jesus, Son of David, have mercy on me!' 1.41 And he had pity on him. 8.23 And when he had spat (in his ears) and laid his hands upon him, he asked him, 'Do you (hear) anything?' 7.35 And his ears were opened . . . and he (heard) plainly. 5.34 And he said to him, '(Son), your faith has made you well; go in peace and be healed of your disease.' 5.43 And he strictly charged them that no one should know this. 5.20 But he went away and began to proclaim in the Decapolis how much Jesus had done for him. 1.27 And they were all amazed, so that they questioned among themselves, saying, 'What is this? A new teaching with authority.'

Participation in a shared text-world, here in the 'world' of miracle stories, makes the process of tradition possible. The same is true of understanding. Understanding is addressed not only to the individual intention of the author but to the shared text-world which the individual author actualizes, constructs or changes in his concrete text. His 'intention' is more than the subjective purpose in the formulation of a text (which is indubitably present); it is a contribution towards the construction of a text-world which transcends the individual – and as such a contribution can be evaluated objectively, without our needing to penetrate the author's inner world.

Let us summarize these first ideas. Any individual biblical tradition which as a rule is the subject of a sermon, is always to be seen against the background of a biblical text-world. It is related to it as a 'parole' is to a 'langue', as a speech act to a collective speech system. Therefore the handing down of an individual text is at the same time a generative process which reactualizes the possibilities of the sign system.

A second notion needs to be added to this.[6] It is not about the relationship between sign-system and concrete text but about the relationship between the vehicle of the sign and the significance of the sign, or the significant and the significate. We saw that tradition succeeds where texts are read against the background of the same cultural sign system. This sign system contains the code by which content is given to the vehicles of the signs (i.e. to the patterns of optically visible letters or acoustically audible sound-waves). This connection is an act of interpretation both for the author (the one who sends the message) and the audience (those who receive it). It is not given by nature, but created by convention. The linguistic significants are thus connected with significates, which in turn relate to the reality that exists outside language (the referent). Thus understanding comes about by connecting interpretations on the basis of a code present in the collective sign-system. This produces a semiotic triangle:

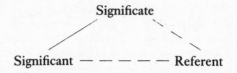

Significate

Significant — — — — — Referent

As in the case of all connections based on human convention, which do not already exist by nature, deviations are possible, disruptions of the connection between significant and significate. A word can be used in a transferred sense which deviates from the usual terminology. The phenomenon is part of everyday language, but appears in a concentrated form in religious and poetic texts. In them, semantic disruptions are deliberately provoked in order to perceive reality in a different way from hitherto, indeed to draw attention to the 'Wholly Other' as compared with our everyday world. Therefore symbols and metaphors are constituent characteristics of religious and poetic texts. They have the capacity to say something new. Their semantic power fades if they, too, become mere conventions, in other words if the unusual element in a metaphor is no longer heard and it is, for example, no longer surprising that the redeemer is described as a 'thief' who breaks into the familiar world by night (cf. I Thess.5.2; Rev.3.3; Matt.24.43).

The linguistic power of religious texts is closely connected with their semantic potential for disruption, i.e. with their capacity to prompt new connections between significant and significate – and here to evoke new meanings. Therefore religious and poetic texts are, more than texts in our everyday language, 'open texts',[7] which challenge the interpretative power of the hearer. Here, too, a collective system of pre-existing meanings is posited: there can be deviations only where conventions are presupposed.

Accordingly, the re-actualization of texts in the process of tradition within the Bible is not just a recall of existing possibilities from a collective sign language, but a constant semantic disruption of pre-existing meanings. It is the successful 'speech events' in particular which reactivate the sign system by semantic disruption. Thus the preaching of Jesus revitalizes two basic metaphors of the Jewish tradition, the metaphors of God's kingdom and of God as Father. Some semantic disruptions of conventional connections are striking here.[8] Traditionally, a victory of Israel over the Gentiles was associated with the kingdom of God. However, for Jesus the Gentiles stream from every corner of the earth (together with the Diaspora Jews?) into the kingdom of God, whereas those who already believed in it are cast out (Matt.8.1of.). Jesus now combines this metaphor of the kingdom of God in an unusual way with the metaphor of the father. While he speaks of God's kingdom, he never (in the words attributed to him) speaks of God as king; i.e. he describes the power of God as 'kingly rule', but not his person as 'king'. Rather, the metaphor of the father replaces the metaphor of the king: God comes to power as father. Therefore the first Christians say, 'Our Father... your kingdom come!' In this unusual combination of metaphors there is an evident transformation of the notion of power which we hardly notice any more because we are so familiar with the linguistic imagery of the Bible.

In this way I have sketched out a model (albeit an incomplete one) for the process of tradition within the Bible. It is a reactivation of the biblical sign system in ever-new texts which does not simply reproduce the collective sign language but provokes new insights and attitudes by measured semantic disruptions.

I want to transfer this model of the process of tradition within the Bible to the process of tradition which comes about in present-day preaching. In order to do this, I must define the character of the biblical sign system more precisely. So far I have compared it only vaguely with a linguistic system. The linguistic system of Hebrew and Greek is of course presupposed in the Bible. However, these linguistic systems are claimed in the Bible by a specific sign system, a religious sign language. But what is religion? Or rather, what is a religion?

I would like to propose the following definition: religions are historical sign systems which make possible for human groups an awareness of enhancing life by corresponding to an ultimate reality.[9]

Behind this definition lies the anthropological assumption that human beings are symbolic animals: living beings which live not only in a natural world but in an interpreted world.[10] They could no more live without transforming the natural world into a word of signs than they could survive without a technical transformation of the environment – without clothes, houses and tools. A sign system takes on religious character when it seeks to make contact with an ultimate reality and to enhance and preserve life by 'assimilation' to this reality. The signs which a religion 'appoints' for this are rites, texts (like myths and narratives) and objects – i.e. temples, holy places and images.

When it comes to the Bible and biblical religion we can make this general definition of religion concrete once again: biblical religion is a sign system that arose in history (in the course of around a millennium), which gives Jews and Christians the awareness of entering into dialogue with the one and only God and thus enhancing life. Accordingly the Bible can be characterized by five functions. It is

1. The basis of a world of signs,
2. A storehouse of individual texts (or pericopes),
3. An opportunity for entering into dialogue with God,
4. The promise of enhancement and orientation in life,
5. A means of communication for Jews and Christians.

The Bible has canonical character for the Jewish and Christian religious communities because the whole sign system of Jewish and Christian religion can be reconstructed anew time and again from its text.[11]

The purpose of a sermon is to reactualize the biblical world of signs – in all its functions. Accordingly it has five dimensions:

1. It is an actualization of the biblical world of signs. Here it must bridge the distance between past and present. To this degree every sermon has a *historical hermeneutical dimension*.

2. It is a development of the potential meaning of the open biblical text by a revitalization of its language. The relationship of the sermon to the concrete text of the Bible is its *exegetical hermeneutical dimension*.

3. It is an opportunity for entering into dialogue with God, i.e. it is bound up with the hope that it can overcome the distance between God and human beings. This is the *theological dimension* of preaching (in the narrower sense).

4. It promises enhancement of life, i.e. an orientation which can make life succeed – even if in the event it has often worked, and still works, against its intention. It acts on the distance of human beings from their authentic life, on the alternative of salvation and disaster. This is its *existential dimension*.

5. It is public discourse in the framework of worship, in which a member of the community attempts to formulate the foundations of its

common life as a representative of all its members. It seeks to bridge the distance between human beings. It has a *communicative function*.

We can now attempt a summary definition of the sermon. A sermon is a discourse in worship in which a member of the community, as a representative of all its members, reactualizes the biblical sign language by the interpretation of a biblical text in the hope of communicating enhancement of life by entering into a dialogue with God.

We might compare this with another definition: 'The sermon is Christian discourse which in the context of worship interprets the biblical tradition for its hearers in order to strengthen them in their certainty of Christianity and to further their orientation in life.'[12] Here three dimensions of the sermon are addressed: the historical dimension appears as the task of interpreting the biblical tradition for the present; the existential dimension is stressed twice as the furthering of certainty and an orientation on life; the communicative dimension occurs in the definition of the sermon as 'discourse' in the framework of worship. Remarkably, the theological dimension is well in the background – it is addressed only implicitly. 'God' is mentioned only indirectly in 'certainty of Christianity', in so far as this certainty relates to God. Beyond question any sermon would lack its distinctive element were it not stamped throughout by its relationship to God – though here my concept of God is perhaps too 'big-hearted' (see below).

Otherwise, three special features of my description of what a sermon is (and should be) need to be stressed. First, it differentiates between biblical text and biblical sign system. The biblical texts are regarded as parts of a comprehensive 'sign language': as the expression of a religion. Not only the text but the religious sign system in it – the religion in the depth structures of the text – is essential to my understanding of the task of preaching and to the overcoming of historical distance. I want to go on to demonstrate this.

The second special feature is the definition of the existential significance of preaching: certainty and orientation in life are indeed also an 'enhancement of life', but this last concept is stronger. One could understand certainty and orientation as 'illumination of existence' – and distinguish it from a change of life. The sermon aims at more: at a change of life, at a new creation.

I see the third special feature in the emphasis on the representative character of the preacher. This is essential for the communicative process between preacher and congregation. Preaching is a one-sided process of communication. The fact that good sermons are nevertheless a dialogue with the congregation is due to the fact that the preacher is thinking, formulating, doubting, questioning as its representative.

But perhaps definitions are not decisive; what is more important is the basic notion of the following remarks on preaching, the notion that the biblical sign system is structured by a few basic motifs which D.Ritschl calls 'implicit axioms'.[13]

What is meant by this? In many biblical texts we find formal common features which are presupposed in them as certainties. One example is the basic motif of wisdom, i.e. the conviction that a superior intelligence is invested in creation. We find this conviction in very different genres, e.g. in sentences which draw attention to regular connections in reality, in admonitions which call for a life in harmony with the ordering of the world, and in mythical-sounding narratives about the wisdom which seeks recognition among human beings. The basic motif is always the same. Time and again it is presupposed that a superior wisdom is hidden in surrounding reality, of which human wisdom is only a reflection. Therefore this wisdom can be spoken of in an 'objectifying' way, by personification and as a hypostasis. Wisdom is the object of human striving and longing. She encounters human beings as a 'person', as an imperative and a promise to seek and find her. She is finally elevated to the status of hypostasis, a partial aspect of God which in a playful way becomes independent alongside God.[14]

The inhabitants of the biblical sign world infer from all these concrete statements less a doctrine about reality than a motif for dealing with this reality. In the light of the motif of wisdom they decode their experience in order to make ever new discoveries of a superior wisdom of creation – and also have the experience that wisdom is concealed under its opposite. What looks from the outside like 'folly' can from another perspective be superior wisdom.

As we shall see later, there is a wealth of such basic motifs which we pick up by hearing biblical narratives and meditating on biblical images in our 'hearts'. They are learned, and are thus *a posteriori*. But once they have been learned and internalized, they act as an *a priori* of thought, perception, feeling and action. They form a network of expectations with which we order our experience and guide our axioms.

The great variety of basic biblical motifs can be derived from a meta-axiom: from the First Commandment. The whole sign system of biblical faith has its centre in it. It is organized, unified and shaped exclusively by it. For the First Commandment contains a denial of all gods and deities alongside the one and only God. It contains within itself the claim that in the sign language of biblical faith everything is in the last resort determined by it, so that this sign language has a tendency to constitute itself as a self-organizing sign system.

The meta-axiom of biblical faith has two fundamental aspects: God appears in the First Commandment on the one hand as the God of deliverance, who led Israel out of servitude in Egypt, and on the other hand as the God who makes demands, who forbids the worship of all other gods. God appears as grace and demand, indicative and imperative. For Jews, both are contained in the Torah, for Christians in the figure of Christ.

These two aspects occur in all basic biblical motifs. The creation motif contains an indicative, that it is good that the world exists, and at the same time an imperative – human beings have the task of preserving their world. This twofold aspect of is and ought, grace and demand, promise and claim, runs right though the biblical world of signs.

However, this biblical sign language with its great variety of motifs does not encounter us as a formulated system, but in a wealth of narratives and images, in many concrete texts. The distinction between basic biblical motifs and concrete biblical texts in my view makes it possible to specify the task of preaching in all its dimensions. Before I go on to that in detail, here is a brief sketch in anticipation.

1. The historical dimension. The knowledge of a few basic motifs can contribute towards bridging the distance between past and present. In my view, above all these basic motifs in the Bible can claim validity today, but not the concrete (often mythical, legendary) statements in which they have been formulated.

2. The exegetical dimension. Preaching refers to biblical texts as 'open texts', the potential meaning of which is developed first in the great variety of interpretations. However, this great variety of interpretations does not lead to arbitrariness. All of them must be checked by the concrete text. All must be presented in the framework of basic biblical motifs.

3. The theological dimension. If the First Commandment stands behind all these basic motifs, it means that in any sermon everything can be related to this commandment explicitly or implicitly. If preaching is not an opportunity for making contact and entering into dialogue with God, then it is just talk.

4. The existential dimension. If all the basic motifs are experienced

as promise and claim from the centre of the symbolic language of faith, we find the enhancement of life and the orientation which preaching is supposed to communicate: it promises human beings unconditional value as the image of God – and commits them to a life in accordance with this status.

5. The communicative dimension. The basic motifs are convictions which have been learned. We are not born with them, but to different degrees have grown into them. In my view, preachers attain representative significance where they perceive and interpret their own lives and conduct in the light of these basic motifs. In this way their subjectivity can take on representative character, even if they themselves are still unfinished and must grow in faith through crises.

I

Preaching as an Opportunity to Actualize the Biblical World of Signs: The Historical Hermeneutical Dimension of Preaching

The exegesis of biblical tradition for the present does not take place only in preaching. Exegesis also takes place in lectures, commentaries and monographs. All these genres are about an understanding of the Bible. However, preaching is about something more. Here the hearer is meant to come to an understanding with the Bible, to belief in the 'unconditional concern' of these texts. Understanding presupposes identification.

Nowadays this understanding must establish itself in the face of four reservations. It is not a naive understanding, but an understanding achieved after misunderstanding and indeed rejection. First of all it must establish itself against two historical reservations.

The first reservation is that so many improbable things are said in so many texts that in principle they cannot be true. We are confronted with miraculous events and with non-human subjects. Angels and demons intervene in history. There are myths. A voice in us says, 'It can't have been like that'.

The second reservation is even about texts which seem quite credible and whose content remains in the sphere of the plausible. But they, too, are sources capable of error, written by people who were capable of error. So we hear a second voice saying, 'It could have been like that, but it could also have been different.'

Now the Bible not only contains texts which intentionally report historical events (though central theological statements are bound up with the history). It also contains parables, paraenesis, arguments. But here, too, involuntarily objections arise, two further hermeneutical reservations which we should not underestimate.

The third is that the texts come from another world which is alien to us. Their ideas are antiquated, but above all we encounter values and norms which often seem repugnant to us. Many women (and not only women) find some patriarchal statements quite intolerable. Again a voice from the congregation says, 'But that's all very strange and remote' (or should be remote, as in the case of patriarchal statements).

The fourth reservation is not based on the hermeneutical distance between past and present but on the hermeneutical conflict between a reading of the text 'from above' and one 'from below'. Isn't there much illusory comfort in the Bible? In our quartet of voices which accompany preaching the last whispers, 'But all this is childish wishful thinking, or the religious cosmetics of a repressive reality'.

When we preach, we should be aware that we are adding our voice to a concert of discordant accompaniment. In the present day, no one can simply silence these voices which accompany preaching. But how are we to cope with them?

Two answers leave me dissatisfied, even if they contain an element of truth. The first answer identifies the hermeneutical distance between the text and the present prematurely with the distance between God and human beings. We must put up with strangeness of the text (its improbability, its questionableness) because the kerygma itself is strange: God is wholly other. Dialectical theology tends to give such an answer. The correct insight here is: when we come upon offensive texts, shouldn't we ask ourselves why they are so offensive? Perhaps they are telling us an unwelcome truth. Could, for example, the widespread antipathy of liberal Protestants to the vicarious death of Christ be connected with the fact that it expresses the all too brutal truth that all life lives at the cost of other life? If one argues like this, one discloses in the text not the strangeness of God, but the strangeness of human beings to each other.

The second answer takes the opposite direction, even if it is often given against the background of 'dialectical theology'. The sceptical voices which accompany preaching will be intensified because the text may fail as a historical or literary phenomenon, so that the wonder that God speaks through such questionable texts appears all the greater. In a sentence: the text is buried by historical criticism in order to rise in the kerygma. The correct insight here is that we should take seriously the fact that texts which have been gnawed at by decades of historical-critical storms and winds have not yet been eroded. However, perhaps we should not immediately see this as a miracle of the Holy Spirit but try to interpret the texts in a more loving way. Perhaps we have buried historical criticism all too hastily.

Both solutions are unsatisfactory. Whether the kergyma is now incarnate in the historical and hermeneutical strangeness of the texts or paradoxically rises from the ruins of historical strangeness – in both cases the possibility of our coming to an understanding with biblical texts is underestimated.

The question in my view is not whether or not we identify ourselves with the biblical texts as a whole, but with what we identify ourselves in these texts. Here traditional hermeneutics likes to resort to the intention of the author – often to the 'real' intention of the author, as opposed to its time-conditioned expression in the text. But in biblical texts we are often confronted with 'several authors': a text which appears in all three synoptic Gospels possibly has a different intention for each of the evangelists. And as it is the result of a lengthy process of tradition it has many authors: all the tradents who have left their traces in it. Even in the case of Pauline texts the 'author' is not always completely clear. It could be that Paul himself collected fragments of his letters to form new ones.[1] The original intention of Paul and that of Paul editing his own letters need not have been identical.

With what can we identify in the texts? To that I would want to give the following answer. We can identify more easily with the depth structures of biblical texts than with their present form. The secret of preaching consists in creating new texts with the material of the literary elements and structures that we find in the Bible, from the basic structures of biblical religion. Such sermons are not just expositions of the biblical text (an exposition in the classic sense would be more of a limit case of such a reproduction of the text), but variations on the biblical text which to some degree presents the theme.[2] But now we come to these depth structures of biblical texts.

A. Basic motifs of biblical faith as the generative foundation of preaching[3]

The language of Christianity is traditional biblical language. Just as there are attempts in philosophy to replace the languages which have grown up in the past with an 'ideal language' free of the defects of everyday language, so too in theology there may be a longing to replace biblical language with a purged theological language. It will not prove successful. It is more promising to discover more order and logic in the 'languages' that are actually being used than to develop new languages in accordance with a particular 'logic'. Any language (including languages that have become 'disorderly' and historical) is governed by a few rules which everyone who uses it learns unconsciously. Only a few 'grammarians' raise them to consciousness, just as only a few theologians raise the basic norms of biblical language to consciousness. We internalize them unconsciously when we hear biblical texts and accept them in 'our hearts'. Anyone who comes to faith interprets life and reality in its light. They are communicated historically, tied to the letters – and yet as little identical with the letters as a grammatical rule is with the concrete sentences which are formulated with its help. These basic motifs of biblical language are the spirit of the Bible.

I shall now give an open list of such basic motifs. They will never be finally formulated.[4] Nor do they form a strict system, but more of a loose structure of rules with overlaps and points of contact, like a mobile which is always in movement and yet contains a hidden structure.

1. *The motif of creation*. Everything is as it were created from nothing. Everything could also not be – and be different. The divine power which creates from nothing is active at every moment and enters history in the resurrection of Jesus from the nothingness of death.

2. *The motif of wisdom*. The world is made by God's wisdom, which shows itself in the improbable structures and beauty of the world but which is often also concealed under its opposite – to the point of the 'folly' of the cross in which God's wisdom is radically hidden.

3. *The motif of miracle*. All sequences of events in the world are open to surprising changes; nothing is fully determined. God and human beings, faith and prayer, bring about remarkable changes. Jesus is the bearer of such miraculous power.

4. *The motif of hope*. A growing promise runs through history – leading to the expectation of a new world which has already begun in the midst of the old world. Now human beings are citizens of two worlds, imprisoned with their 'sarx' in the old world but with the 'pneuma' obligated to the new world that has begun with Jesus.

5. *The motif of conversion*. Individuals have the possibility of radical change. Just as the world must change to accord with God's will, so too must human beings: they can begin a new life, if they allow themselves to be crucified with Christ and enter with him into the gift of a new life.

6. *The exodus motif*. Not only individuals but whole groups are changed by God's call – beginning with the exodus of the clan of Abraham from Mesopotamia, Israel's exodus from Egypt and the return of the exiles from Babylon, up to the dawn of the New Testament community in a new world as disciples of Jesus.

7. *The motif of faith*. God discloses himself through human beings whom we trust, i.e. not primarily through material structures, institutions or notions but through a 'You' whom we encounter in a free relationship of trust without any compulsion. At the centre of all human beings through whom God speaks to us stands Jesus of Nazareth.

8. *The motif of incarnation*. God is really present among human beings and in the world – in Christ, in the word, in the sacrament and in every believer through his Spirit. He hallows everything through his presence. The incarnation in Christ makes this nearness of God to human beings certain once and for all.

9. *The motif of representation*. Life is representative life for others: either a life of unconscious suffering, at the cost of which other life develops – or conscious life for others which sacrifices itself for the sake of others. The bloody sacrifice of animals bears witness to the pressure to enhance life at the cost of other life. Christ shows the alternative: life as self-surrender for others.

10. *The motif of changing position*. The first will be last and the last first. That is how Christians should behave in the community. That is also how God acts in history, above all in Christ. The judge is judged, the priest becomes victim, the ruler of the world becomes a slave. But the crucified Christ becomes the foundation of new life.

11. *The motif of agape*. Every fellow human being becomes a neighbour through love – whether through the quest for the lost one who has moved away from the community or through the acceptance of the stranger who is remote from us or the love of the enemy who hates us. Here, too, Christ is the image of such love; his surrender of his life is love of those who were God's 'enemies'.

12. *The motif of self-stigmatization*. A message is contained in suffering voluntarily undertaken or affirmed: a testimony to the truth, whether through asceticism or by taking on the role of a despised outsider, or even through martyrdom. A transforming power emanates from those who are supposed to have been subjected. Christ is the great model of such transforming power through voluntary self-stigmatization.

13. *The motif of judgment*. All life is subject to selective processes. Only human beings are aware of this: they know that they are threatened – not only as physical living beings but also as moral agents. They are measured by what they have done – by ethical criteria, according to which God passes a final judgment on them. The criterion and the judge is Jesus.

14. *The motif of distance*. No life corresponds to the ultimate reality which has brought it forth and sustains it. In human beings, this

remoteness from God becomes conscious and is radicalized by the experience of guilt and suffering. Both these separate human beings from God. In Christ, God himself takes part in this distance, discloses it and overcomes it.

15. *The motif of justification*. The legitimation of existence is as unfathomable as the existence of life itself. It is ultimately a creation from nothing which human beings receive, just as they are receptive to their physical existence. They have created nothing themselves. The foundation of justification is the new creative action of God in Christ.

I see the 'spirit' of the Bible, through which faith illuminates the world and which has taken form in Christ, in such basic motifs.[5] In my view such basic motifs make it possible to build a bridge from the Bible to our modern world. These motifs may not be identical with the basic motifs of a modern secular consciousness, but they do have parallels in it. Such parallels make it possible also to interpret the world of biblical convictions for outsiders – not necessarily with the aim of making them inhabitants of the biblical world of signs. A good deal has already been achieved if outsiders value the 'house' of biblical images and narratives: understanding is not immediately agreement. But it can become agreement at any time. So I want to indicate astonishing analogies in the present secularized consciousness, some of which of course can be explained by the fact that the modern world has been persistently shaped by Judaism and Christianity:

The motif of creation is matched by the awareness of the contingency of all things.

The motif of wisdom is matched by the 'regularity' of the world which is presupposed in all sciences.

The motif of miracle is sometimes matched by a decided 'indeterminacy': trust in the decisiveness of chance.

The motif of hope is matched by a utopian awareness which exerts pressure towards changing the world.

The motif of conversion is matched by a therapeutic awareness which thinks it possible to alter behaviour for the good.

The exodus motif is alive in a different form in the manifold liberation movements of modernity, e.g. in the workers' movement, the youth movement and the women's movement.

The motif of faith is matched by a humanistic 'culture of encounter'.

The motif of incarnation is matched by the modern drive towards the bodily concretion of all that is spiritual.

The motif of representation can link up with the modern awareness that all living beings take part in the same living stream.

The motif of a change of position is alive in the anti-authoritarian attitude of the modern world.

The motif of agape is matched by a secular solidarity which deliberately includes strangers.

The motif of self-stigmatization can be encountered in techniques of provocation and demonstration in the modern world.

The motif of judgment finds an echo in the awareness of personal responsibility – if not before God, at least before one's own conscience.

The motif of distance is matched by a fundamental awareness of absurdity – to the point of the modern 'disgust' of human beings at themselves.

The motif of justification is matched by the conviction of the unquenchable dignity of human beings – independently of their actions and their transgressions.

What distinguishes these 'secular' analogies from basic biblical motifs is that all biblical motifs are related to God. Those who experience and interpret life and reality in the light of them come upon an abundance of meaning to which their lives are merely an echo and a response. By contrast, a secularized consciousness must understand such basic motifs as human schemes which owe themselves solely to human creativity.

A secularized consciousness also interprets 'God' as the result of human creativity – possibly even with a certain respect for religion: as a help towards great control of emotions, an impulse towards altruism, and so on. A religious consciousness in turn interprets the secularized claim as illusory: what is alleged to be free human self-development is a response to a challenge. But we shall be discussing this in the chapter on the theological dimensions of preaching. Here we are concentrating on the historical dimension, the overcoming of the distance between the past and the present.

The reference back to basic structures is not enough by itself. Our sermons would become tedious if their essence could be given in fifteen points. To use the model of language once again: the grammatical rules of a language are limited. But with their help we can make an unlimited wealth of statements – and time and again formulate new propositions. And it is the propositions that are interesting: someone who has mastered French grammar need not yet have read French literature. The concrete texts are more than the basic structures which underlie them. The same is true of biblical 'language'. The concrete biblical texts are the material of preaching.[6] It is formed from them.

B. Consequences for the shaping of preaching: biblical texts as a field of variations in preaching

A sermon does not seek just to be a grammar lesson in biblical language, but to be a piece of biblical language itself. In order to be able to speak a language, it is clearly not enough just to know the grammatical rules by which words (lexemes and morphemes) are linked. Rather, one has to have a certain vocabulary with which one can constantly formulate new statements according to existing rules. Here such a 'vocabulary' in the wider sense includes not only words but also phrases, formulae and patterns of text. Now if we regard religion as a kind of language, i.e. as a sign system with a specific grammar, a knowledge of the basic motifs is not enough either to live in this language or to give it new life. Rather, we have come to know these basic motifs in, with and under concrete complexes of signs. We have grasped them intuitively – from biblical narratives, from rites (like baptism and eucharist) and sacred objects, e.g. images and buildings. The religious sign system embraces linguistic, performative and substantive forms of expression.[7] And just as one can speak a language very well without being able consciously to formulate its grammatical rules, so we can also grow into a biblical sign language without clearly giving an account of its basic motifs. However, when communication is disrupted, it makes sense to go back to such basic motifs – just as in linguistic problems we sometimes reactivate our grammatical knowledge.

Now the bridging of the historical gap between past and present is bound up with disruptions in communication. So it would make sense to define the hermeneutical task of preaching by saying that it creates new texts with the material of our modern 'sign world' – i.e. with words, images and convictions which are familiar to us – on the basis of biblical motifs which remain the same. Here the basic motifs would seem to be timeless constants and the concrete material of the text in the present a historical variable. But that is not the case even with the decisive aspects of a language: grammar is not timeless, but alters in the long term. Vocabulary certainly changes very much more quickly, but always by picking up and developing the traditional store of words (and similarly the traditional store of text-structures, types of text and genres). The same is true of religion: in the long term the basic motifs change their character. Conversely, the concrete forms of expression are often very much more persistent than many people think. The decisive thing is that both processes of change take place in continuity with the traditional sign system. Without that there would be no Christian identity.

So I would plead firmly for connecting sermons closely to biblical texts and images, but making this connection the foundation of a creative, indeed playful, process. The elements present in the biblical texts are to be restructured, varied and organized into new texts on the foundation of the basic biblical motifs, which lie deeper.

Such variations on biblical texts can pick up particularly well the imagery and narrative aspects of biblical texts. In accordance with two basic forms of religious imagery I would distinguish variations of metaphor and symbol, and in accordance with two aspects of narrative texts, variations of role and action. In the end every text is a communication between an author and an audience. Author and audience can also vary, i.e. be replaced playfully and fictitiously by others. This gives us six possibilities of homiletical variations, and they do not exhaust all the possibilities.

1. *Variations of metaphor.*[8] A metaphor is a semantic disruption, i.e. a combination of meanings in the text which either have at one time deviated from 'normal' expectations (as is the case with conventionalized metaphors) or still do so (as with living metaphors). So a metaphor is never an isolated word or an isolated meaning but arises only through their combination in a text. It is a textual phenomenon. The biblical image of 'fruits of repentance' is a metaphor because fruits normally grow only on trees and bushes – and so we have expectations of a similar combination in a text. These expectations are corrected. Behaviour also brings forth a fruit. The semantic break between 'fruit' and 'conversion' is at the same time a signal that we are not to understand this combination of words literally. No one has the idea that those who change their behaviour literally bring forth fruits of the change – with, say, bananas growing out of their noses!

In the Bible we find not just individual metaphors but whole metaphors and fields of images.[9] In other words, the individual metaphors are embedded in images which are related in content, which are not actualized in the text at all but are virtually present as substantive alternatives. Brief mention should be made of three great fields of imagery:

(a) Nature and vegetation metaphors in which the vegetation metaphors can be divided into two partial fields of imagery: 'tree and fruit' and 'seed-growth-harvest'.[10]

(b) Substantive metaphors like 'house', 'vessel', 'ship', 'temple', i.e. human artefacts which become partly an image for a community ('house of God') and partly imagery for the individual ('temple of the body').

(c) Social metaphors, which occupy a central place in the Bible: God is the Father, and the Israelites and Christians are God's children. 'Wisdom' appears as God's wife. Human beings are God's workers.[11]

Because such metaphors release a wealth of substantive associations (and already in biblical times only 'functioned' in the context of such associations, i.e. within their field of imagery), it is appropriate to use these associations for preaching. The metaphor of the house necessarily suggests the notions of different rooms in a house – only the houses of very poor people had just one room. The parables about the returning householder presuppose large houses with many servants. So we can develop this idea of the different rooms: in one and the same house there are richly decked dining rooms and torture chanbers in the basement; sick rooms and festal halls; rooms where people go to relax and others where hard work is done. There are rooms of joy and rooms of suffering. And all the inhabitants are occupied in either forgetting these contradictory parts of their houses or creating a balance between them. In so doing all relate to the master of the whole house, for whom the house forms a unity, even if its inhabitants forget its cohesion.[12]

Thus by the elaboration of the elements present in it, a metaphor leads through the actualization of hidden oppositions and the use of relevant imagery to little 'parables', narratives of a fictional kind in which reality is often depicted more aptly than in abstract descriptions. The presupposition here is always that the metaphor is not understood literally. The world is not a house. But human society can be compared with a house.[13]

2. *Variations of symbol*.[14] In contrast to a metaphor, a symbol must always also be understood literally. It is misunderstood only where perception is limited to its literal meaning. Thus the cross is primarily a specific form of gallows by means of which Jesus was executed in the first century CE. But this cross has taken on additional meaning in becoming part of a comprehensive history of God and human beings in the form of a history of enmity and rejection – and of reconciliation, peace and forgiveness. The cross takes on its additional symbolic value

Biblical texts as a field of variations 25

by being embedded in this comprehensive history. That applies *mutatis mutandis* to all symbols and symbolic events. They can be understood literally. But they take on additional value as part of a comprehensive story. In the view of the evangelists the withered fig tree really did stand before the gates of Jerusalem (and possibly there was such a fig tree which gave rise to various explanations of why it had become withered). However, in the framework of the Gospel it takes on a symbolic meaning: it demonstrates that the leaders of Jerusalem do not bring forth the fruits which God expects of them.

Symbols can be varied by being put in new contexts – here every context is as a rule a narrative. Such 'narratives' into which we order our life have different ranges: our individual life is a narrative context, human history is an immeasurably greater one, the epic of evolution the greatest possible narrative context that we know. The more comprehensive context always contains the smaller one within itself. The same symbol can often take on additional value in all three contexts.[15] This is shown by the example of the scapegoat in Lev.16, which is one of the great symbols of the Bible.

The most obvious context is the history of the community, for we meet the ritual of the scapegoat in Lev.16 as a rite of atonement. The transference to the context of our present society is not difficult: all societies tend to foist their own tensions and unsolved problems on 'scapegoats', usually on defenceless minorities who are made responsible for the shadow side of life.

But we can also put this ritual in a cosmic context. Biological evolution is based on the fact that less adapted forms of life have lesser chances of life (i.e. lesser chances of survival and procreation) than others. Without the principle that the 'weaker' life ('weaker' in the sense of less fit) is 'sacrificed' in order to make enhanced life possible, the development of life forms would be inconceivable. We arrive at the scapegoat ritual when human beings deliberately stage what takes place unconsciously in biological evolution – either in reality (by destroying competing life) or in a ritual depiction of such destruction. As long as we stage scapegoat rituals we are still 'caught' in the principles of biological evolution.

A third 'narrative' context for the symbol of the scapegoat is individual life. In the scapegoat ritual two goats are sacrificed: one is offered on the altar for God, the other is sent into the wilderness laden with the sins of the people. Such a process gains additional symbolic value as the account of a process which takes place in every human being: time and again we are occupied in sacrificing part of our energy for valuable aims (offering it to God in 'reasonable worship'), but sending other parts of our energy into the wilderness, i.e. repressing them or deliberately suppressing them. The ritual vividly presents us with the need to create an equilibrium betwen two processes – sublimation and repression.[16]

So whereas metaphors turn into narratives and thus become parables of life, symbols come to life if they are embedded in real contexts or, to put it more cautiously, in what are really believed to be contexts. For of course such a context can also be a myth. The inhabitants of the myth take it to be real, but others regard it as fiction.

3. *Variations of role.* Images (whether metaphors or symbols) become fruitful in narrative texts. They can be varied in them. But the basic structures of a narrative also allow variations. Thus in any narrative a series of persons or subjects occurs who usually appear in typical roles: as hero, antagonist, companion, spectator. The narrator can adopt different perspectives on them:[17]

– The perspective of the omniscient narrator who is equally detached from all the persons and can empathize equally with all of them.
– The perspective of a person by whom all the others are perceived.
– The perspective of an observer who knows all the persons only from the outside and learns about their inner life only from what they say.

A favourite variation of role in existing narratives consists in a change of perspective. The same story is retold from the perspective of one of those involved: e.g. the trial and condemnation of Jesus from the perspective of Pilate or one of the soldiers or of one of the high priests making the accusation. Such a change of perspective consists in one of the different figures appearing each time in the role of the 'narrator'.[18]

The external course of the story can remain the same in such a change of roles. Nothing need change. Yet everything appears in a new light. Paul himself shows how such a change of roles can motivate insight: he asks the Corinthian community to put themselves in the place of an outsider who comes into the community and meets a wave of incomprehensible glossolalia. Won't he have to conclude that they're mad (cf. I Cor.14.23)?

As an example of a variation of role and its great homiletical value, here is a reformulation of the darkest anti-Judaistic text in the New Testament, John 8.43–44, which describes the 'Jews' as children of the devil.[19] I shall preface it with two remarks to show that my variation of the text takes its depth structure (i.e. the presuppositions implicit in it) very seriously. This is a reformulation of the surface structure of the text which retains its depth structure.

1. It is important that the text asserts not that the Jews *are* children of the devil but that in particular circumstances they have *become* so. Really they are children of Abraham. But when they killed Jesus they came under an alien power: under the power of Satan.

2. The material reason for the charge of being children of the devil is a particular form of behaviour: killing a messenger of God. The implicit premise is that those who kill people who speak God's truth are not doing their own will but that of the devil.

So on the basis of the premises contained in the text one can say: those who kill human beings who communicate the truth of God to others are doing the dark work of Satan and thus are taking his place in the age-old history of murder. In the present text of John these implicit premises are explicitly applied to Jews because and in so far as they kill Jesus. Today, after a long history of the persecution of Jews by Christians, we are far more justified in applying it to Christians: Christians have constantly killed Jews or allowed them to be killed, although they knew that Jews are witnesses to the God in whom they too believe. Now as the Johannine text is addressed to Jews who have become believers, it can also apply to Christians. Through role variation we then arrive at the following text:

> Jesus says: 'I know that you are my followers. But you seek to kill Jews because the word of God is making no progress in you. I speak what I saw with the Father, but you are doing what you heard from your father.' The Christians say to him: 'We are not inauthentic children of God. God is our father.' Jesus says to them, 'If God were your father you would love the Jews. For like me they have come from God and still come from God; they did not come of their own accord, but God has given them a commission to bear witness to him in the world. Why do you not understand that? Because you cannot hear this commission. You come from the devil as your father and want to do the will of your father. He was a murderer of human beings from the beginning and did not stand in the truth. For the truth is not in him.'

A change of role need not necessarily involve a change in the whole action. But if e.g. a subsidiary person becomes a main figure, the variation in role will usually also turn into a change in the action itself. That brings us to the third possibility of textual variation.

4. *Variations of action.* Everyone knows the intellectual game with history which goes 'What if?'. What if Caesar had not crossed the Rubicon? What if Pilate had not condemned Jesus? When history takes

place it is open to many possibilities – at least for those involved, who do not know how it will go on. Only in retrospect does it often seem necessary: 'It had to happen.' But even in retrospect, toying with those possibilities which surround the reality has an important function: it sharpens the perception of what really happened and what it could have meant. Sometimes the New Testament texts themselves contain implicit references to such possibilities. In the conversation about paying tax, one of two possible answers is expected from Jesus. First, it is forbidden to pay taxes to the emperor because God alone is Lord of the land. All its produce belongs to God. The emperor has no right to it. The second possible answer could be: it is God's will that taxes should be paid to the emperor. God has allowed him to rule the land. In the end God himself stands behind the emperor's rule. The point of Jesus' answer, 'Render to Caesar that which is Caesar's and to God that which is God's', only becomes clear in the light of these two possibilities, which are not realized. It becomes clear that the widespread 'conservative reading' of these maxims does not get to their original sense. There is no formulation of a religious obligation to pay tax.[20]

Variations of action are conceivable not only with 'real actions' (in which we could also include 'speech acts') but also in fictional genres, in similes and parables.[21] Four variant actions are conceivable in the parable of the prodigal son. I shall mention only one of them: the prodigal son comes back from abroad, by no means on his beam ends but with a fortune. He returns as a rich man, marries a rich woman and has many slaves, much property. Yet he is still the prodigal son, since he has denied the principles that he learned in his father's house to acquire his riches. He has howled with the wolves, and lost no opportunity to enrich himself at the expense of others. Such a variation on the action fits a Central European congregation much better, since such a congregation usually contains well-to-do people. Even without moral aggression one can hold up a mirror to one's hearers by such variations on the text, and show them that it is about them. Insights which are communicated in such an indirect way lie deeper than insights with which people are confronted as finished results.

5. *Variations of author and audience.* One could list far more possibilities of variations on the text in preaching. I shall limit myself to two examples: every biblical text has an author and an audience. This can most easily be seen from the texts of letters, but it can also be seen in prophetic sayings. Of course one can also vary such authors and audiences.

A variation of author might consist in putting the same text on the lips of someone else. The maxim 'Love your enemies . . .' sounds very different depending on whether one gives it to a member of the upper class who has not much to fear from his enemies (or can even utilize his enemies for his own interests by the shrewd employment of power) or whether one puts it on the lips of an insignificant person – or even makes it the statement of someone who is persecuted, humiliated and despised.[22]

Variations of audience can consist, for example, in reformulating Jeremiah's letter to the exiles – each time to different audiences: to people in the present who are aware that they have been banished from a certain 'security' in nature; to Christians who feel foreigners in a secularized society – and to every individual banished from childhood. Here are three variations on the symbol of 'exile' – combined with a variation of audience.[23]

That should be sufficient illustration of the principle of variations on texts. Time and again it is a matter of speaking from the Bible, not about the Bible. Speaking from the Bible means using basic biblical motifs as the grammar of a language which consists of biblical metaphors, symbols, roles and actions. The link to the basic biblical motif thus makes possible a much freer play with biblical language. By variation on this biblical language it is possible to speak about the present without giving rise to a homiletical gap between then and now, and without that disastrous division of sermons into an exegetical section in which one refers to all the difficulties in the text and then a section orientated on the present which is largely detached from the biblical text.

I can now sum up these reflections on the historical hermeneutical dimension of preaching. The gulf between the biblical past and the present cannot be bridged by theologically drawing attention to the gulf between God and human beings – or by a theological devaluation which welcomes the archivistic remoteness of the text in order to be able to understand a preaching which brings it into the present as an even greater miracle. In both cases the distance between past and present is bridged not with the help of the biblical text but despite the biblical text. The biblical text is not expected to become open to the present through intensive work.

Here I want to show a way orientated on the Bible which is not biblicistic or fundamentalist: biblical texts are an expression of a biblical sign language which is governed by a few basic motifs as its grammar. These basic motifs are usually grasped intuitively. Those who have read their way into the world of the biblical text will be familiar with them, even if they cannot formulate them explicitly. But it is the task of the theologian and preacher to raise such basic motifs to consciousness. The more these basic motifs become a certainty for preachers which guides them in living and in interpreting the world, the more freely preachers will be able to 'play' with texts and elements of the text of which biblical sign language consists. Fidelity in basic matters makes freedom in the concrete shaping of the sermon possible.

It is a sign of such freedom when the imagery and narrative elements of the text become a field of variation for preaching. The biblical text is not simply repeated, but a new text is formulated on the basis of the fundamental motifs of biblical faith with the help of the biblical language which is present in it. The preacher becomes the co-author of the biblical text which he or she creates anew from their presuppositions. The sermon is from the Bible, not about it.[24]

Without doubt that is a 'liberal' way of dealing with the text while at the same time being bound to it. The preacher is free from the letter and documents this freedom by producing free variations. But all this happens for the sake of the Spirit which speaks from the Bible. Here competence in biblical language and symbolism is required of the preacher. To make biblical texts the field of variations for preaching, preachers must be capable of actualizing virtual images and narrative elements which are only potentially present in the text of preaching but which belong to the world of the biblical text.

One could now ask: why shouldn't the preacher be content with a 'scope', a single point? Why not only present the concrete text but also bring to life the world of the text? Why lead the community into a world of possible meanings? There is a clear answer to this. It happens for the sake of the freedom of the hearers. They are not being guided towards a single point but are shown alternatives. They themselves decide on their point. What we have deliberately decided lies deeper in our lives that what we have appropriated without any alternative.

To this degree it can be said that the variation of biblical texts is the expression of a 'liberal' way of dealing with the text of the Bible. The preacher is freed from the letter. Preachers document their freedom by producing free variations on the text, and give their hearers freedom to appropriate it in the form of one of these variations. But all this takes place for the sake of the Spirit which speaks from the Bible. The specific biblical text is appropriated in this spirit – as a result of the free decision both of the preacher and of the hearer.[25]

II

Preaching as an Opportunity to Develop the Open Text: The Exegetical Hermeneutical Dimension of Preaching

Sermons always relate to specific biblical texts. These texts are more than a storehouse of images and narrative patterns with which the preacher can work. They are the reference texts of preaching. So one would think that in homiletics there should be an unassailed primacy of exegesis.

This primacy of exegesis once existed, but it does so no longer. For various reasons a farewell has been bidden to it in reflections on homiletics over the last thirty years.[1] The primacy of exegesis was closely bound up with the proclamation homiletics of kerygmatic theology. If the biblical texts contain the word of God, a precise grasp of the text must have precedence over everything else in preaching. With the retreat of kerygmatic theology, other factors came into the foreground: the homiletical situation, the effect of the sermon, its rhetorical character, the personality of the preacher. It is legitimate to ask: aren't these as important factors for the content and form of a sermon as the biblical text itself? Aren't these the factors which determine whether a sermon reaches its hearers? Mustn't exegesis necessarily lose significance if the supreme aim is for the sermon to find hearers?

In addition to this shift of interest from the text of the Bible to other factors, two motives came into play to dethrone exegesis in homiletics.

In a concern to analyse the present situation, the hearers, their action, and so on, categories of historical criticism which have been learned are of little use. Wasn't it more natural to hope for enlightenment from disciplines orientated on the present, from communication theory, psychology, sociology, etc.? In this way the gulf between past and present came to be deepened by different methods and categories. For different languages are being spoken in each case.

A second reason lay in the 'scope' method. This gave the domination of exegesis in preaching a particularly narrow form. The 'scope' was the point of the text, its central intention. The customary instructions were to work out this point through exegesis, to formulate it into an impressive statement and then translate that into homiletics.[2] The text was to dominate in preaching by means of the 'scope', and exegesis was to be an instrument of this domination – and at the same time the supreme judge. For it had to decide on which 'scope' was right and which wrong.

The homiletical rebellion against the primacy of such exegesis was understandable, but one-sided. The defenders of the exegesis rightly remarked that the exegesis kept the preacher from another domination, that of the public.[3] Or, on the basis of a long experience of preaching, it called for 'biblical' preaching among other reasons because preaching otherwise would become sterile.[4]

All this is correct. But the argument should have gone on the offensive even more. As long as sermons are texts on biblical texts, exegesis has a regulative function for every sermon. What is to be called for is a new primacy of exegesis. That cannot be a return to the old domination of exegesis in homiletics. For Bible and exegesis have lost their old claims to that.

The Bible no longer has the unconditional authority it had in the days of kerygmatic theology. Preaching enters into a dialogue with the Bible, but does not submit to it. However, even in a dialogue it is all-important to understand one's conversation partner precisely; otherwise the dialogue becomes a monologue.

Now the exegesis of a past text is a dialogue only to a limited degree. The text cannot protect itself against unfair exegesis. The author cannot react to abuses by exegetes. Precisely for that reason, a disciplined exegetical method is necessary. Only it can representatively put in a claim for the text against its premature appropriation.

But, many people will say, isn't the procedure of this method itself a violation of the text? Isn't the text often taken apart in intolerable scholasticism, stored in archives of the past, removed from living usage? Doesn't exegesis result in the domination of the academic community and their administration of the cultural heritage?

What a caricature of exegesis! Present-day exegesis is quite unsuitable for laying claim to domination. It is increasingly being recognized that religious and poetical texts are 'open texts'. They allow a number of interpretations. They have ambiguous potential meanings which can be developed only by the interpretative activity of readers and hearers. There is no one sacred interpretation. There is not even one 'scope'. What we have to bid farewell to is not the primacy of exegesis but the primacy of the one 'scope' provided by the biblical text.

Furthermore, for a long time exegesis has made use of categories which are akin to the elucidation of what happens in preaching today. Communication theory, linguistics, sociology and psychology have found their way into exegesis, albeit to very different degrees.[5] And conversely, it is dawning increasingly on scholars that the social sciences have a false consciousness of themselves if they suppress the historicity of their object and of their theories.[6]

A new primacy is required for a new exegesis, for exegesis which constantly opens up new approaches to the biblical text, an exegesis which self-critically makes use of the categories with which we also analyse our life in the present, an exegesis of 'open texts' which challenge the interpretative activities of readers and hearers.

The first section of this chapter will sketch out in what way the text is 'open'. The sketch of an 'analytical hermeneutics' is meant to show how the recognition of an open text does not surrender its exegesis to arbitrariness. On the contrary, it seems arbitrary today for open texts to be interpreted in such a way that hermeneutically they are fully determined.

In the second section we shall be concerned with the pluralism of methods, forms of reading and approaches to the Bible. This pluralism is an opportunity for preaching. The old experience of preachers is confirmed anew: that one can preach on the same texts time and again and yet discover something quite different in them each time.

Finally, I shall comment on the formal shaping of sermons as texts on texts: homiletical commentary on texts is something different from scientific commentary. Anyone who argues for the primacy of exegesis is not arguing for sermons as miniature pieces of academic exegesis.

A. The Bible as open text

The discovery of the open text was prepared for by many tendencies in exegesis and literary criticism. It arose first from the ever-increasing pluralism of methods and approaches. If one does not want dictatorially to give one method a monopoly, one is forced to recognize that the texts allow different interpretations, methods and forms of reading. Three new hermeneutical approaches and insights have encouraged this insight: the history of the influence of texts, the evaluation of the reader in modern theories about readers, and the simultaneous relativization of the intention of the author.

In many forms of exegesis the history of interpretation is treated as the prehistory of exegesis proper. But it is more. If the meaning of a text is also constituted (and not just shifted and distorted) by the preunderstanding of the reader, then one can also regard the history of interpretation as a diachronic development of the meaning of the text – and not just as an approach to a meaning of the text which all interpretations can attain only approximatively. The history of interpretation then becomes part of the history of the influence of the text (which as a whole is more comprehensive than the history of interpretations). The text develops in it. It must then be consistently integrated into exegesis.[7] However, anyone who recognizes various successive interpretations in the past as the development of the meaning of a text will, to be consistent, also accept different interpretations existing side by side in the present as developments of the meaning of the text with equal value.

At the same time modern theories of reading attach greater importance to readers. Their preunderstanding is constitutive for understanding the text. It not only distorts the meaning which is handed down but also discloses it. The pre-understanding (i.e. the understanding of the text which is always already conveyed with it) influences the final understanding; the partial understanding has an effect on the understanding of the whole, and the understanding of the whole in turn has an influence on the understanding of the parts; the understanding of the context changes the understanding of the text, which appears in a constantly new light by being put in new literary and historical contexts. The pre-understanding is often regarded one-sidedly as a historical given to which individuals have a passive relationship. Here the reader seems to be determined by his or her contingent historical situation. By contrast, modern theories emphasize the activity of the reader.[8] To be understood, the open text depends on the action of the reader, which gives it meaning. The reader has a share in creating meaning. Here it is open how far the text guides this activity of the reader (how far as reader he or she is 'implicitly' in the text and has only to enter into a given role) or how far other factors also influence the activity of reading: the community of readers with its traditions and norms, the experiences of the reader, and – last but not least – his or her free insight and creativity.

Probably all four factors are involved, so that in the understanding of the text both the text itself and tradition, experience and insight play a part.

This revaluation of the reader is matched by a simultaneous relativization of the author. The aim of traditional exegesis was to grasp the author's intention. Strictly speaking, however, that can relate to authors only in so far as they have entered the text with their intentions. The author is present in the text as 'implicit author'. This 'implicit author' has to be distinguished from the real author. Even if the real author interprets his or her work subsequently, this interpretation does not *a priori* have greater importance than other interpretations: an author can often give only an incomplete interpretation of a work. The work has a relative autonomy from its author.[9] This relativizing of the author is familiar to theological exegesis. In pre-modern biblical hermeneutics the human authors of the biblical writings were instruments of the Holy Spirit, the real author of scripture. In modern biblical hermeneutics the authors often became more or less chance mediators of age-old currents of tradition. What the last author says is at the same time governed by the many authors of the previous history of the tradition, by stores of genres and formulae which have been handed down, by collective fields of words and images. To this degree the 'dethronement' of the author is nothing new for biblical exegesis. Here perhaps the opposite needs to be stressed: the implicit author must have something to do with the real author (who is often unknown to us).

However, the decisive factor is not how the concept of the 'open text' came about but what constitutes the open text. In other words, what is so open in the text that it has to be formed by the activity of reading for the text to be understood? Here the old distinction between a syntactical, a semantic and a pragmatic dimension in the text is helpful, even if it cannot be carried through consistently. The text is first of all a fabric of different statements which are linked together 'syntactically'. Secondly, a text has a semantic dimension. The signifiers of the text (the physical patterns which can be perceived optically or acoustically) are given a content which relates to the outside world. Thirdly, the text is part of a pragmatic transaction: an author has formulated it for a particular audience with the intention of having a definite effect.

In all these dimensions the reader must 'add' something for understanding to be possible. These additions are not made arbitrarily. Many are required by the text itself – and here these demands of the text are always communicated through social conventions and traditions. But no convention is so determinative in human life that it does not allow variations. In it is recorded the history of the individual experience of the reader. Here the reader become creative and joins in creating the meaning.

The text has an openness in its syntactical dimension. It is rarely possible to divide it without making decisions, not to mention locating it in the context of other writings. There are always several possibilities for division. The same goes for the selection of central passages: even if the given text is the same, we emphasize different sections as being important depending on the way in which we focus our attention. None of these structurings of the text (in its syntactical dimension) is independent of the content of the text. Suppose we take the parable of the prodigal son as an example. It has two climaxes, two points. It is up to readers whether they see the centre in the conversation between the prodigal son and his father or in the protest of the older son. Or they may see in the relationship between the younger and older sons a (latent) point which is not followed through.

In the semantic dimension every text is more or less open at a quite elementary level. We are given only the physical signifiers. Any assignation of a content to them, any link between the significant and the significate, is carried out by the hearer and reader on the basis of linguistic and cultural norms. Here texts leave a good deal open. M.Leiner has drawn attention to three basic ways in which we supplement our reading.[10] We visualize: we vaguely imagine the 'best garment' which the prodigal son is given on his return home. Before that we envisage a ragged form, although the text says nothing about this. Furthermore we 'historicize' in narrative texts: we add sequences of actions and processes which are not explicitly contained in the text. The ending of the parable of the prodigal son is deliberately left open. Finally, we 'psychologize', i.e. we attribute motives and feelings to those involved. This may be in a very diffuse and unclear way, but we cannot avoid doing so. It happens automatically. So it makes a difference whether we see the younger son setting off for a life of dissipation – or into a freedom in which he comes to grief. The text says nothing about his motives. There is a void here. Finally, the whole story is a parable. Texts with imagery put particular demands on the interpretative activity of the reader. The literal sense of the text is still relatively clearly indicated by linguistic and cultural norms. By contrast the transferred sense is ambivalent, based on a semantic disruption, a measured deviation from conventional usage. What this deviation seeks to say is left open; its meaning still has to be discovered. Symbols and metaphors are stimuli for readers to find out for themselves how far the image corresponds to what is meant. To what extent is God a father? To what extent is God not a father? Images and symbols make us think; they do not excuse the reader from thinking. That is why they are so valuable for human life.

In the pragmatic dimension there is no mistaking the degree to which we must supplement by interpretative activity in order to be able to understand. We now have the texts from the past in decontextualized form. The author is no more accessible to us than are the first hearers. Often we do not even know precisely where and when a text was written. For example, was the Gospel of Mark written at the centre of Roman power, in the capital, Rome? Or in some remote place in the province of Syria? Even now we cannot decide. Historical criticism to a large degree consists in restoring a context to texts which have been recontextualized in the process of tradition, i.e. in reconstructing the author, situation, audience and ideas of the author and the expectations of the recipients. However, in addition to this historical recontextualization there is a present re-contextualization in the reading: the text as we now have it has an effect on the reader. In narratives, readers will always identify with a variety of figures (by way of experiment).[11] Whether and how they do it governs their attitude. Here the texts are open. In the parable of the prodigal son, for example, should we identify with the son who returns? Or the son who stayed at home? Or even with the father who behaves in an almost offensive way towards the 'failure': instead of welcoming him and giving him a chance, he honours him in an incomprehensible way.

Biblical texts are open texts. And instead of complaining that exegetes do not provide any clear reading, but are constantly proposing new readings, we should be delighted: a religious text is all the more valuable, the greater its potential meaning. Preaching lives by the fullness of meaning in biblical texts. It is therefore unfair to complain about the masses of hypotheses that we exegetes produce about the texts. These hypotheses are an expression of the overwhelming potential meaning in biblical texts, and they contain much that is valuable for sermons.

We can therefore draw the provisional conclusion that the fact of the open text cannot be denied, and texts are open to different degrees: a religious and poetical text is more open than a set of instructions. In religious texts, the quest for the one sacred interpretation is over. One can react to this situation in different ways. Postmodern hermeneutics interprets the detachment of interpretations from a definite pre-existing meaning as liberation; in the end everything is then equally valid and becomes a matter of indifference. The traditional hermeneutic implicit in the humanities often refuses to derive the openness of the text from its structure: for this hermeneutic, the phenomenon of the open text is the consequence of our inadequate knowledge and our incomplete methods. This produces a strong impulse to develop new methods and procedures, in order to reduce randomness and indifference. Depending on the philosophical tradition and the basic ethical attitude involved, answers will thus turn out differently. The postmodern hermeneutics of interpretative freedom is a training in tolerance; traditional hermeneutics motivates towards ever more differentiated methods of gaining knowledge. Each has an element of truth in it.

My own hermeneutical principles lie between these two poles. They can be classified as the kind of 'analytical hermeneutics' which M.Leiner has sketched out as the possible basis for a text-psychological exegesis.[12] Here I shall content myself with a brief sketch in the form of five theses.

1. On the relationship between the discovery and the creation of meaning in understanding. All understanding has a constructive element. In order to understand, we must always put into the given text things that it does not contain. We must supplement it. Without such 'inferences', i.e. connections and pieces of information which are put into the text, we do not understand anything. Therefore a plurality of interpretations, methods and approaches is unavoidable. For the inferences called for by the text cannot clearly be defined.

2. On the relationship between understanding and testing. No interpretation can be derived from the text 'inductively', but every interpretation has to be tested by the text. If usually there are several permissible interpretations, there are also illegitimate interpretations which one can reject in a reasoned way through comparison with the text. So interpretations can sometimes be clearly falsified, but can be verified only approximatively – though here we cannot rule out alternative interpretations.

3. On the relationship between individualizing understanding and generalizing explanation.[13] Understanding is directed towards individual circumstances which can only approximately be grasped in general terms. But this understanding depends on explanation, i.e. on the knowledge of universal rules and norms which applied in the culture in which the text came into being. This knowledge of the rules, i.e. the knowledge of ethical, religious and literary norms, is a knowledge of

universal contexts and norms. In contrast to the knowledge of laws in the
natural sciences, in the historical sphere it relates to a limited section of
history. Above all, norms are not automatically realized in history: there
is no cultural norm without the possibility of breaking it or evading it.

4. On the relationship between understanding and application.[14]
Contrary to the prevalent view of existential hermeneutics or a
hermeneutics focussed on the history of the influence of a text,
understanding does not take place through identification and
agreement. We can understand texts with which we do not agree on the
basis of our convictions and values. We can put ourselves in the position
of people who are motivated by different axioms from us – to the point
when we say, 'We too could have spoken and thought like that had we
shared their world.' In all this we are not taking over alien value
judgments and convictions. Rather, the culture of understanding begins
where we understand without being in agreement, and we can also look
at what we are in agreement with from the outside – from the perspective
of another. So methodical understanding should make e.g. the text of
the Bible accessible independently of whether someone is a Christian or
not, and independently of whether he or she wants to adopt the attitudes
of the Bible as part of a way of life.

5. On the relationship between understanding and evaluation.[15]
Texts potentially have the power to transform. They can change people.
So we have an obligation to develop an ethic of dealing with texts. If texts
can gain such great power over human life, we should not accord just
any texts this power over us. The criterion is clear at one point: where
texts have caused suffering we must interrupt their influence. Certainly
we can understand such texts and make them comprehensible, but we
should contradict them if we want to prevent them from influencing
lives.

B. The many different approaches as an unfolding of the open text

The legitimacy of a pluralistic approach to the Bible derives from the
insight that the Bible is an open text.[16] Its potential meaning can only be
developed by a variety of approaches. Nevertheless interpretations are
not random. On the one hand they have to be checked by the text and
can be rejected as unfounded. On the other hand, methods of procedure
have developed within the various approches which limit arbitrariness.

They are the expression of lengthy experiences with biblical texts – including bad experiences of inappropriate dealing with them.

For the sake of simplicity, three approaches can be distinguished: the methods of academic exegesis, committed forms of reading and practical forms of communication. This division is not fortuitous. It corresponds to the domination of exegetical competences which were already distinguished in Protestant orthodoxy as *subtilitas intelligendi*, *applicandi* and *explicandi*. And it corresponds to the three relationships between text, interpreter and interpretative community. That needs to be explained briefly.

Many hermeneutical reflections seem to presuppose only a twofold relationship: understanding and interpretation are seen as a relationship between a text and its interpreter. But a third factor is always present (at least potentially): the community for which the interpreter acts. As a rule one interprets a text for other people – for a school class, a university seminar, a community, a college. Those to whom the interpretation is addressed need not always be present. Someone sitting alone at a desk writing a book on interpretation still always has a particular group of readers in view.

In this triangle of interpretative relationships the different capacities of interpretation are challenged to different degrees. First of all the interpreter must understand what a text is saying. That calls for *subtilitas intelligendi*. This is dominant in the direct relationship between text and interpreter – although it is considerably furthered by a conversation between several people about a text. Scientific methods primarily further this process. They seek to discover the meaning of a text. But the community is usually not so interested in the subtleties of understanding; it wants to know what the text means for it pragmatically. What conclusions are to be drawn from it? What effects does it have? What limits does it set? This calls above all for *subtilitas applicandi*, i.e. the competence to use a text in such a way that past meaning becomes motivation for present conduct and experience. All committed forms of reading are an expression of this. In them the exegete is active as the member of an interpretative community – and not so much as its critical counterpart. This brings us to the third relationship in the triangle of interpretative relationships: the relationship between the interpreter and the community for which the interpreter is active. Here above all there is a call for communication in the sense of a capacity to explain an acquired truth for others in such a way that it is really important for them. The practical forms of communication (regardless of whether they seek more to communicate the results of scientific methods or the stimuli of committed forms of reading, are expressions of this *subtilitas explicandi*. This gives us the following picture:

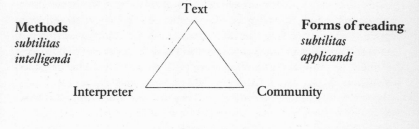

Text

Methods
subtilitas
intelligendi

Forms of reading
subtilitas
applicandi

Interpreter   Community

Forms of communication
subtilitas
explicandi

However, this scheme should not be pressed. Methods serve to disclose the text appropriately; but they are also rules for dialogue in discussions of the text. Despite their orientation on application, forms of reading have a power to disclose the text. Practical forms of communication do not just explain what was known without them; where they are used in the service of aesthetic shaping they often have their own power of disclosure. They are a heuristic reservoir for new insights into texts and new possibilities of applying them.

1. Scientific methods

A wealth of new approaches has been developed in the last thirty years in order to understand biblical texts better. In addition to the classical methods of textual and literary criticism, form criticism and redaction criticism, two groups of new methods have appeared. On the one hand there are methods in which the Bible is taken seriously as text and literature; on the other there are methods in which it is interpreted as an expression and factor of wider areas of life: as part of social and psychological life. Often exaggerated hopes for hermeneutics have been associated with all methods – above all the hope of snatching ancient biblical texts from their past and bringing them nearer to the present. If we look closer, however, we shall find that in most approaches there is a tension between greater proximity and distancing, i.e. those methodical procedures which make it possible to grasp texts in their historical context and leave them there, without directly putting them in the context of the present.

Text-critical approaches have often been shaped by the hermeneutical longing of structuralism to discover in all textual worlds universal structures which remain the same, structures which apply as much to Russian fairy tales as to the modern novel and the Gospels.[17] The quest is either for fundamental binary oppositions, for elements of action which remain the same (like trial, deliverance, catastrophe, resolution, etc.), or recurring configurations of persons (e.g. hero, opponent and adjuvant). Correspondingly, one can distinguish between a binary, a functional and an actantial structuralism. The decisive point of hermeneutics is that despite the distance in content between the ancient text-world and the modern world in which we live, the aim is to discover 'orders' of actions and persons which remain the same or are at least analogous, by recourse to the depth structures of texts. However, an exegesis inspired by structuralist notions need not necessarily lead to the disclosure of universal structures. It would in fact already be valuable to elucidate historically limited structures in the texts and convictions of the New Testament. Relatively constant basic motifs of the biblical sign world would be helpful. So these structural elements need not be understood already as supra-historical. On the contrary: they have become historical, are preserved by cultural tradition, and can change. The view of earliest Christianity sketched out above, as a sign world guided by a few basic motifs, cannot be imagined without the stimulus of structuralism, but it does not share its philosophical premises, i.e. the assumption of timeless universals.

Methods of literary criticism[18] can be distiguished from related text-critical approaches in the narrow sense by the way in which they take seriously the 'poetic' quality of the text. They include such complex matters as fictionality, imagery and perspectivity. Here biblical texts are analysed like literary works. In one respect, methods like literary criticism, narrative criticism, etc. have a clear advantage over the classical exegetical methods: they investigate the final form of biblical texts, i.e. the influence that these texts have had in history and the influence they still have in religious life today. Those looking for the religious content of biblical texts have therefore often emphatically welcomed these holistic approaches. The aesthetic relationship to the text is comparable to the religious relationship – especially in the case of an enlightened form of religion which takes account of fictionality and poetry in the biblical text. But here, too, in academic interpretation there is a counter-movement of distancing: we can investigate the holistic effect of texts on the reader both in the context of the past and in that of the present. Which context is chosen makes a big difference. Thus for ancient hearers and readers the biblical text was certainly not 'poetry'. It was simple 'truth'. And the readers responded to the texts with basic anxieties and hopes which are remote from the present world of Western and Central Europe,[19] in contrast to that of Latin America, Africa or Asia.

As a rule, text-critical and literary-critical approaches work within the texts. Both orientate themselves on the coherent text in its final form. Its formation and its influence barely come into view. But precisely that is the case in sociological and psychological exegesis. While these begin from texts, they understand these texts in the context of life as a whole. They re-contextualize the text.

In sociological exegesis, too,[20] whether consciously or not, the hermeneutical longing for an approach to the text is alive. It is often shown less in the form of sober sociological analyses than through committed exegesis which has discovered an inexhaustible potential for emancipation in the great religious texts of the past – provided that one reads these texts critically and against their use in church, which often domesticates them. Social kerygmatic exegesis in particular found an impressive social message in the biblical text – a support for any rebellion against compulsion and repression.[21] Both the exodus from Egypt in the Old Testament and the dawn of the kingdom of God in the New have been interpreted in this sense. But here, too, scientific exegesis led to distancing. On modern premises we would need to see a religion shaped by the exodus as an outcry against any form of slavery. But the fact is that in the Bible, as throughout antiquity, slavery was taken for granted, even if for Israelites it was limited to temporary slavery for debt and was in principle to be abolished in the sphere of the Christian community (Gal.3.28).

Psychological approaches are least 'established' in the canon of the new scientific methods.[22] That is understandable, since there are few convincing examples here. And here, too, first of all the hermeneutical desire to get closer to the text dominated. The archetypal exegesis of E.Drewermann is characteristic of it.[23] Here all biblical texts appear as timeless imagery for God and the unconscious in which the great drama of the human self on its way to wholeness is depicted. The exodus from

Egypt becomes the exodus from neurotic compulsions. Again (as in structuralism) we find recourse to timeless and universal structures – this time not to structures of the text but to 'archetypes', i.e. deep structures of human behaviour and experience which appear in the images of dreams, myths and fairy tales. But here, too, scientific reception led psychological questioning to distance itself again. It is no coincidence that one of the most interesting contributions to psychological exegesis appeared under the title *Historical Psychology of the New Testament*, with the programme of demonstrating that human behaviour and experience in antiquity was different from modern experience and behaviour – and evades the grasp of modern psychological methods and theories.

If we compare the two groups of new scientific approaches, in recent discussion the literary-critical approach has often been felt to be nearer to theology. One of these approaches even calls itself a 'canonical approach'. Conversely, sociological studies are often felt to be a continuation of historical research as a reading of the biblical texts 'from below' which has a scant relationship to a kergymatic reading of them 'from above'. Appearances are deceptive. Both approaches can be combined with theological commitment: both can have a reserved attitude towards it. Anyone who enjoys biblical texts aesthetically can neutralize their religious content, like an atheist who enjoys Bach cantatas as an expression of human emotion. Compared with aesthetic distancing, historical and sociological works on the Bible are an indispensable reminder that these texts stand in an living setting, that in them suffering and fate, conflict and hopelessness, are coped with in a religious way. Both groups of methods can work in both directions: distancing and bringing closer to the text.

Nevertheless, the impression that sociological and psychological approaches can come abruptly into conflict with the self-understanding of religious texts in a way which is hardly conceivable in the case of text-immanent and literary approaches is not totally false.[24] They do not offer only an interpretation of texts, but above all an interpretation of the religion expressed in these texts. In the classical theories (in Marx and Freud), there is an impulse towards the criticism of religion which is part of the everyday awareness of educated people. In short, these approaches 'from below' lead exegesis into a 'hermeneutical conflict'. Are they therefore less valuable for the preparation of sermons? Should preachers keep more to literary interpretations of the text as a distinct world – because these interpretations correspond more to a religious self-understanding? To that I would want to say a clear 'no'. Critical distancing from the basic texts of our religion (and also the texts of other religions) has now become a key ingredient in the understanding of religion: coming to an 'agreement' with these texts in a way which goes beyond understanding is always a matter of overcoming or rejecting a conflict with the texts. It is a 'Yes' after or despite a 'No'. Preachers who in dealing with the texts have themselves experienced the power of this 'No' which is so critical of religion can also convincingly formulate the post-critical 'Yes' to them. On behalf of the community they go through the distancing in the critical conflict to the point of a new post-critical agreement. In their intellectual work they witness what moves many of their hearers semi-consciously: anyone who evades the hermeneutical conflict evades the present.[25]

Of course sociological approaches are important for preaching, even independently of their explosive power in the criticism of religion. For the criticism of religion is not a necessary part of the method of such approaches, but rather part of the philosophy of some of their representatives, and one need not adopt this philosophy along with the methods which it inspires.[26] Often even the criticism of religion becomes virulent when it is a question not only of theories and interpretations but of practice: of social aims (or utopias) and personal schemes which are beyond question contained in the psychotherapeutic schools of our century. In short, the criticism of religion becomes virulent where science becomes committed knowledge – whether in the social sciences or in exegesis.

2. *Committed forms of reading*

We have seen that scientific methods can bring about both a greater nearness to the text and a distancing from it. To the degree that they bring greater nearness, they can be combined with committed forms of reading. Nevertheless the latter are distinct from scientific methods. In committed forms of reading greater nearness to the text is a programme. They do not seek to be either remote from application or open to identity; their aim is to utilize biblical texts for social and individual life in the present and to make Christian identity possible. It is characteristic of them that they are all potentially at a critical distance from scientific methods because they reject distanced and 'objectivizing' influence. They are a source of the necessary criticism of knowledge.

In committed forms of reading, again two groups can be distinguished. Some are governed by the principle of hope: they seek an ally for a liberating praxis in the Bible. Others are governed by the principle of faith. Here the basis for (true) faith is sought in the Bible. This faith need not necessarily be traditional Christian faith, as in the evangelical reading of the Bible. It can also be the modern form of faith. In my view, existentialist interpretation and its keygmatic-theological interpretation of the Bible are committed forms of reading.

(a) Bible reading in the light of hope

The most important forms of reading correspond to the three polar groups mentioned in Gal.3.28: Jew and Greek (i.e. Gentile), free and slave, man and woman. The difference between Jew and Gentile is the theme of Jewish-Christian reading of the Bible,[27] the difference between free and slave of the form of reading in liberation theology and the social kergyma,[28] the difference between man and woman of feminist reading of the Bible.[29]

The issue here is always liberation: liberation from the pernicious traditions of anti-Judaism, imperialism, patriarchalism. Behind these forms of reading stands the principle of hope. Many present a kind of hermeneutical messianism. They promise redemption with the Bible, but also the redemption of the Bible from the hand of particular opponents.

The three forms of reading mentioned above are characteristic of the development of biblical hermeneutics after the end of the debate on demythologizing. That debate was about the interpretation of ancient ideas for modernity: faith and understanding was the great theme of this time. The new forms of reading are engaged in a critique of biblical norms and values: faith and conduct is the decisive theme. And that is an important difference. Whether or not we understand the Philippians hymn with its poetical Christ-myth literally does not affect our moral integrity. But that integrity is affected if we find ourselves in traditions some of which can lead to Auschwitz. No one can quietly allow that to rest. So the debates in committed forms of reading are carried on with great moral commitment, and often are morally overloaded.

Scientific exegesis usually has a reserved relationship to these forms of reading. But it makes things too simple for itself if it supposes that the Bible is merely being instrumentalized and given a different function in them.

The values by which the various forms of reading are governed often have roots in the Bible: in them God is in fact concerned for Israel; God often takes the side of the poor. Women seem amazingly free in it. There is no doubt that some sympathetic social involvement can claim parts of the Bible for itself as allies.

Furthermore, the function of committed forms of reading in providing a basis for identity comes close to the original function of biblical texts: they, too, aim to have an effect on life, to provide support in limit situations, to give hope and overcome distress. One often detects more of the spirit of the Bible in committed forms of reading than in much scientific exegesis.

(b) Bible reading in the light of faith

Criticism of committed forms of reading by academic exegesis is also unjust because established exegesis itself is a mixed body of scientific exegesis and a special form of committed reason. It is a coalition which has almost come to be taken for granted, between a reading in terms of kergymatic theology and scientific methods – a combination which was very fruitful for decades. But this combination can by no means be taken for granted. It has become historical. We should recall that the kerygmatic theological reading was experienced at the beginning of dialectical theology as a rejection of scientific methods.[30] Originally it was as much protest exegesis as Jewish-related social kerygmatic and feministic exegesis is today.

The reading of the Bible in terms of kerygma theology which underwent a renaissance after Karl Barth's *Commentary on Romans* was a repudiation of the historicism of liberal theology. This had contented itself with giving a historical account of what the biblical authors had thought one of the presuppositions by which they had been governed. What was said differed widely. At least one is constantly amazed to come across committed theological statements in liberal theology which do not at all match their alleged historicism. Nevertheless, there is no doubt that the text of the Bible stands at the centre of interest as an expression of human faith. But the kerygmatic theological reading sought to advance from this text to the subject-matter on which faith is orientated. It was not primarily interested in what Paul once thought about God but about how we are to think about God today with Paul. Or more precisely, about what God has to say to people today through the letters of Paul.

This kerygmatic theological approach entered into a firm alliance with form criticism. The stability of the combination of the kerygmatic theological reading and scientific method is rooted in this alliance. In the variant presented by Dibelius, form criticism taught that the texts of the New Testament are shaped by an interest of earliest Christianity in preaching: they seek to proclaim God's eschatological salvation.[31] Anyone who reads them again for the content of their proclamation and seeks the message of God in them is thus corresponding to an intention of the texts themselves, which can be established with profane methods.

Thus kerygma and literary form entered into a close symbiosis in the New Testament. This led to an increasing awareness of the tension between kerygma and mythical statements in these texts. This tension led to Bultmann's programme of demythologizing: if the texts are also to become living kerygma today (in accordance with their original kerygmatic intent), this kerygma must be distinguished from its time-conditioned mythical form of expression.[32]

In my view, the exegesis of kerygmatic theology is clearly a committed form of reading. It is not remote from application but aims at application. It seeks to show that our concerns are at issue. It is not open to identity but aims at Christian identity. It seeks to change people, so that they move from an inauthentic life to a true life.

Here we need to mention yet further committed forms of reading. Fundamentalist and evangelical readings[33] belong here, strange though it may seem to mention them alongside Bultmann's existentialist interpretation: in both cases we have a reading of the Bible in the service of faith. In the one case it is in the service of a modern faith which seeks to make itself comprehensible in the present by developing a critical hermeneutic. In the other it is in the service of a faith which is afraid of modernity, which is defensively safeguarding itself against the tribulations of secular thought.

(c) Bible reading in the light of love?

But – one might ask – is there any exegesis at all which is free of interests? Is there an alternative to a committed reading? Isn't every way of dealing with the Bible committed in some way – even academic exegesis, as has just been demonstrated by the example of existentialist interpretation?

The question is a justified one. However, I would want to contradict the obvious resignation that science cannot arrive at reliable results because we are always governed by interests and premises. That would be to miss the opportunity of emancipating ourselves from our interests and premises. This opportunity is based on four factors: 1. on the discipline of method in science; 2. on hermeneutical reflection in which we become aware of our interests; 3. on reciprocal criticism in the academic community: where one has an ideological blind spot, colleague XY has a keen eye. Finally, mention should be made of 4. the history of research, which provides our results with findings which were achieved under quite different historical circumstances. So no exegetes escape their finitude. No one can be completely free of his or her own interests and premises. The stream of history carries all of us along. But science makes it possible for us to change from being swimmers carried along by the force of the current into sailors who can cross even against the current and the wind – though without being able to do away with the dynamic of the current.

However, that is only the first part of an answer. The decisive second part is that scientific exegesis should understand itself in one respect as a committed form of reading. It should combine itself with a strong power which can also impose itself against vital interests. It should be a reading of the Bible in the service of love, for love is hermeneutically superior to faith and hope.

If we interpret biblical texts in the light of Protestant faith, almost two-thirds of all New Testament texts will be treated in a very loveless way. Of the four Gospels, the Gospel of Matthew is thought to be all too imperative, the Gospel of Luke all too historical and the Gospel of John is suspected of docetism. Most of the letters after Paul are devalued with the term 'early Catholic'. Only Paul survives the critical gaze of exegesis; and even he does not always seem to maintain the level of his own insights. Wherever exegesis is driven methodically only by a standpoint of faith, i.e. from the centre of a kerygma or from the 'middle of scripture', there is the danger of a sublime violation of the texts. So I would plead that the texts of the New Testament should first of all be loved in their contradictoriness, without being evaluated in accordance with criteria of faith.

But love is also superior to hope hermeneutically. Those who hope for a better world, in which the poison of antisemitism has been overcome, in which possessions are divided fairly and the opportunities for men and women are more symmetrical than they are now, can see and illuminate many texts of the Bible in a new light with the spark of hope. But they risk overlooking the dark sides of the Bible, or reading the Bible only in the light of a particular theme. Love includes the capacity to allow the many sides of others to stand, including their dark sides – even their prejudices and mistakes, without necessarily approving of them. Love takes into account the limitations and finitude of its counterpart. It tolerates a great deal without giving up sympathy with the text. It also tolerates the contradictions in the texts and the contradiction between the text and its own existence. It is not envious because people of past times were not yet at the level of our insights.

But what is the relationship of such a hermeneutic of love for the text to that reserved ethos of science, which defines exegesis as an activity remote from application and open to identity?

In my view, this reserved scientific exegesis is itself the application of a basic human value without which scientific exegesis loses its identity. Every form of human expression needs to be understood for its own sake. For human beings are never exclusively means, but also ends in themselves. Understanding is a value in itself. This basic hermeneutical axiom is one of the conditions of a good society. Scientific exegesis should be committed to this axiom. Here it should itself become a 'committed form of reading'. Here it represents something humane and indispensable. Here it can become a form of love. For love is the supreme form of doing justice to the self-value of others.

So I come to the conclusion that love is hermeneutically superior to faith and hope. If I had only faith, so that I could move even the remotest text from its historical framework into the sphere of eternal truths – and had no love of the texts, my exegesis would be worthless. And if I had all hope, so that I could bring to expression the unrequited longing for liberation in even the most reserved texts – and had no love for people, my exegesis would be worthless.

It is true of all academic exegesis that we known in part. We look into an open text as into a mirror. We always arrive only at a plurality of readings and exegeses. There are three basic hermeneutical attitudes, faith, hope and love. All three are legitimate. All three will remain legitimate. But love is the greatest of them.

3. *Practical forms of communication*

Alongside scientific methods and committed forms of reading orientated on application there are practical forms of communication which above all require the capacity to present a subject and explain it to someone. The general knowledge which is contained latently in the text in the collective store of knowledge or the possibility of application only comes to life if it becomes personal human knowledge.

These practical forms of communication are not a mere appendix to the 'higher' forms of approach to the Bible. Rather, they often have a fertile effect on methods and forms of reading. What is disclosed, for example, in meditation on the Bible, in the creative retelling of its stories or in the artistic shaping of its content can be a tremendous impetus towards new knowledge or the discovery of new possibilities of application.

Conversely, no scientific knowledge is disseminated without appropriate forms of communication. Every member of the academic world knows that: scientific knowledge must be presented in a particular form if it is to have an effect. It must be published in the right journal or series; it must have an aura of scholarship and be developed in the right way: with preliminary remarks on method, intermediate relativizing comments and wise conclusions. The practical forms of communicating scientific exegesis are not without their shadow sides: empty formulae are often confused with a concern for stylish presentation, incomprehensibility with profundity. Such forms of communication would be a catastrophe for communication outside the academic world. And even within it they do not just act as a blessing.

However, we need not be interested in that here. For the community addressed by the preacher is certainly not the academic world. It is the Christian community – and beyond that all society. The practical forms of communicating the Bible which are appropriate here are marked by three characteristics: in content they are often an alienation of the biblical text; socially, they are embedded in direct interaction; in terms of medium the whole gamut of aesthetic forms can be found in them.

The interpretation of the Bible as alienation – that should not be one practical form of communication alongside others. It should be possible to perceive an alienating effect in all communication. We saw above that speech events have an effect where measured semantic disruptions draw our attention to new things. The texts of the Bible often seem remarkably familiar: everyone thinks that they already know them. If these texts are really to become a 'speech event' which transforms people, that can come about only through alienation – by satirical parodies, offensive paraphrases, playful anti-texts and so on. Such alienating strategies are important for preaching. Only where preaching lacks surprises and becomes predictable does it lose its power to change.[34]

Just as alienations occur in all practical forms of communication, so most of these forms of communication are bound up with living interactions. There is talk about the Bible. Or there is shared meditation on it. Or there are variations in role play. So it is somewhat misleading for a particular practical form of communication to call itself 'interactional' biblical interpretation[35] – a combination of historical-critical exegesis as an alien experience with an experience of the self provoked by the text. The tension between the two, between subjective projections on to the text and objective conjectures from the text, is utilized both to disclose the text for human beings and to disclose human beings for the texts. This too, *mutatis mutandis*, should take place in all practical forms of communication.

The greatest variety can be seen in the means used by the practical forms of communication. To the degree that these media have an aesthetic character they preserve a value in themselves over and above their didactic aim. The aesthetic cannot be instrumentalized in a didactic way. It remains a surplus.

Literary forms of communication correspond to the three basic genres of poetry: drama, epic poetry and lyric poetry. Bibliodrama takes up biblical narratives in role plays and varies them in an alienating way.[36] Here, too, experience of the self by assuming a role and alien experience of the texts, which do not lose their own dynamic, are interlocked. Narrative exegeses[37] continue what already happened in the Bible: in them an aura of fictionality lies over all historical events. Historical events are surrounded by an unhistorical framework of interpretation. Narrative exegeses make use of new fictional framework texts to illuminate and interpret biblical texts. They recontextualize the texts in a way which can be followed not only by historians but even by those who have no access to historical criticism. By contrast, religious lyric poetry on biblical themes leads to the present: it impresses by its authenticity. The 'I' of the lyrics expresses its thoughts, feelings and fantasies independently of the normative expectations of religious traditions.[38]

It is well known that other forms of communication play a great role in religious life: graphic art and music. They are all of great importance for preaching, and not just because every sermon is given in a liturgical framework which includes music and hymns, architecture and imagery. All these practical forms of communication are important for preachers themselves. They open people up to texts. So they can also open the preacher up to biblical texts. Certainly the preacher does not have every form of communication available in the preparation of a sermon. The decisive thing is that the text of the sermon should be approached in many ways, not only by academic methods and committed reading but also by a meditative openness to the text. It is important that in the period of preparing a sermon the text is so deeply immersed in the everyday stream of consciousness that it is lapped by the experience of a whole life and the undertow of the problems of the present, until the realization dawns that in places the text has its own interpretative pull which illuminates and changes the everyday stream of consciousness.

C. Consequences for the shaping of preaching

Preaching is not a matter of exercising domination. The scope does not dominate the text nor the text exegesis; exegesis does not dominate the sermon nor the sermon the hearer. Nevertheless the text has a primacy. Hearing is both a receptive and a creative process. But the word precedes its creative use in hearing. The interpreter is co-author, but not the main author. Receiving precedes the creation of meaning by the exegete. The primacy of the text in preaching and of exegesis in homiletics means that the text and interpretation introduce conditions which are not random but open up a sphere of possible interplay for active hearing and reading. Independent hearing is stimulated where measured deviations from the accustomed and the expected lead people to prick up their ears. However, measured deviations must be evocative, otherwise they are not perceived as deviations. So every sermon must be concerned both to be evocative and to lead to openness. I shall sketch out briefly two suggestions for producing these two characteristics: the primacy of the text becomes evident in homiletical commentary, its openness in homiletical variation.

1. Homiletical commentary on the text

How can it become clear that the text with its own possibility is being expressed in the sermon? And how can a sermon be prevented from offering a series of open possibilities of which the text is only one among others? First of all, this means that in preaching the text is not only a reservoir of images, ideas and narrative structures; it is the reference text for preaching, its object, its theme. A sermon will be good if it speaks from the language world of the text, but always also speaks about the text. It comments on the text.

Beyond question, commentary on texts in preaching is always in danger of becoming academic exegesis. Thus many preachers dispense with it, arguing that the exegesis is presupposed in the sermon and therefore does not need to be repeated in it. However, in my view the sermon loses its intense relationship to the Bible if one no longer dares to comment in it on the text. The decisive thing is that this commentary on the text should be shaped as homiletical commentary – and not as scientific exegesis.

But what is the difference between an academic and a homiletical commentary on the text? The art of writing a good academic book consists among other things in reporting all that is needed to understand the problem in the form of statements and arguments. It is unimportant whether the author is German, French or Swiss, a man or a woman, sick or healthy, when writing the book. Science 'objectivizes' to the degree that all statements must be understandable without any knowledge of the concrete situation of the origin of the text, the circumstances of the author, his or her anxieties, doubts, hopes. Certainly all such human features need not be concealed, but they belong in the preface. They are not essential to understanding. Scientific texts are de-contextualized texts; the context of the individual life of the author has disappeared from them.

Homiletical commentary is different. Here it is quite decisive that all pertinent arguments on the text should be rooted in a tangible life. Here it can be decisive to say 'this dawned on me when I was in bed sick', or 'I owe this remark to a pupil', and so on. It is also part of this living situation that homiletical commentary takes seriously the fact that in science we are never confronted with a single view, but always with several. The preacher must make sense of them without having the time for a balanced scientific choice between different opinions. In short, homiletical commentary recontextualizes the text of the sermon in the context of the present.

One way of fulfilling the demand for a homiletical commentary on biblical texts in preaching is to put all the exegetical statements in a narrative framework. In this way they appear as the expression of a living relationship to the Bible. There are different possibilities for creating such a 'homiletical commentary framework'. I shall list some of them without any claim to completeness.

1. *An exegetical framework*. The preacher relates how he or she, or a fictional figure, asks a variety of exegetes for their view on the text. In this way various interests behind the questions put to scholars can be

illustrated in narrative form. So too can the attitudes and prejudices of the different exegetes. The decisive thing is for the process of exegetical commentary itself to be narrated.[39]

2. *A biographical framework.* The sermon describes how someone copes with the same text at different stages in life: as a child, a young person, an adult, in old age, etc. Of course, preachers can also choose themselves as examples. However, here too a fictional figure often provides more freedom. This again embeds exegetical views in a living process.[40]

3. *A didactic framework.* Almost all preachers are at the same time teachers. So it is natural to describe the difficulties one had with particular ideas in the text when introducing it in religious instruction. Answers from pupils can be very illuminating.

These three forms of homiletical commentary framework have in common a narration motivated by a direct exegetical interest (or at least the possibility of such a narration). But there are other roles and situations in which people make texts the object of their investigation, their judgment, and the formation of their opinion. Here are some examples:

4. *A journalistic framework.* Journalists report and comment, and often the two run into each other, despite assertions to the contrary. So one could shape, for example, a Christmas sermon by letting various media report on the birth of Jesus – broadsheet, tabloid, political news reports or cultural journal. And of course one can also formulate various commentaries on the event.

5. *A legalistic framework.* Wherever a charge can be formulated, a fictitious court can be set up in the sermon to investigate the case. So one can hold the 'trial' of Cain once again, question experts on what happened and attempt to arrive at a verdict.[41] Of course such a commentary framework can also link directly with history. As Paul was probably executed by the Romans, what he said could be investigated in a fictitious trial, and so on. Any passage in his letter could be part of a charge against him.

6. *An epistolary framework.* Many New Testament texts for preaching come from letters. The most natural reaction to letters is to write replies. Responses can be made to everything in this way. Instead of presenting direct 'exegesis' in a sermon we can choose answers as a fictitious framework for indirect exegesis. How did the Galatians reply to Paul's angry letter? How would Barnabas and Peter have reacted to it? What would James have said about it?[42]

There are certainly yet more possibilites for creating a homiletical framework for exegetical remarks on the text in narrative form, but these few examples should suffice. One objection might be discussed briefly: isn't the preacher hiding behind other commentators if he or she doesn't speak personally, but allows others to do so? Beyond question that is a danger (or – in some situations of communication – also an opportunity). Generally speaking, however, any commentary should be authentic, i.e. should be possible from the perspective of the commentator, and its content should be illuminating. If one allows Paul's opponents to speak, they should appear credible, as Christians who wanted to be as serious Christians as Paul himself. They should put forward a relevant concern. Those who hear the sermon will then soon note that here the preacher is (also) speaking. It is also important for the preacher to speak personally at the end, to emerge from the fictitious play with other roles, address the hearer directly and in so doing take up and echo the contributions of the figures who have been making their comments.

Finally, I should emphasize something rather obvious. Naturally it is also possible to make a homiletical comment on the text without narrative frameworks. This happens successfully in many sermons. The important thing is not the form in which comments are made on a text, but that every commentary should appear as the expression of an attitude to the text – and not as a weighing up of arguments and opinions detached from concrete life.

2. *Homiletical variation on the text*

The re-contextualization of the text by a narrative commentary framework constantly guides the attention of the hearer to the text. It stands at the centre if it is constantly illuminated from different perspectives and provided with living contexts. As soon as one is not just content with a commentator here (though that would be possible in principle), one is introducing into the sermon the principle of variation which we have already discussed in the first chapter.

As an open text, the text of a sermon usually contains several possibilities for use. Certainly preaching can set itself the aim of making the many possibilities of interpretation the content of a sermon. But often there are good reasons for concentrating on a theme, say because the situation requires it or because the congregation should not keep hearing something that it has already heard often before. Many sermons I have heard have suffered not from a lack of ideas but from the use of enough ideas for three sermons – none of them developed properly. So as a rule of thumb it is important to limit oneself to one theme in the text, but to vary the theme in many ways. The limitation to one theme makes it clear that the text presents the theme. The creative activity of the preacher and the hearer will consist in continually varying it. Variations make it clear that the text is an open text. They leave the hearers with the awareness that they themselves may vary the text further.

Variations must be given a shape. That is easy if a sermon text is itself a series of variations. Thus in Rom.8.17ff. Paul conjures up the three-fold sighing and lament which runs through reality: as the sighing of creation, of Christians and of the Holy Spirit. Here a theme with variations already resounds in the text.[43] One can find such a theme in other sermon texts by exegesis. Thus for example the healing of the epileptic boy in Mark 9.28ff. can be read as a variation on the theme of representativeness. The disciples attempt to take Jesus' place in his absence and fail. The father asks on behalf of his son. Jesus' faith is representative of the faith of the father: he has a power which can 'do everything'. The key word 'representativeness' is not contained in the text. However, it is not forced on it, but is latent in it. Thus a sermon would be conceivable which varied this theme in the form of a homily, i.e. an interpretation section by section.

Variations must be recognizable. It is a help for the audience if a leitmotiv – a sentence, an image, a key word – remains the same through all the variations.[44] A homiletical refrain after each variation is also appropriate – not just as an indication of division but as an echo of the same theme. We enjoy variations very much more if we recognize the thematic material which remains the same – both in music and in preaching.

Finally, we should not make variations blindly. Even in musical variations, we have pre-structured expectations of genre. The theme must be played at one point on the strings, at another in crisp staccati, at a third point slowly and meditatively, at a fourth in the minor, and so on. There is also a possible 'systematics' of spheres within which the sermon varies its themes. So I often deliberately attempt to develop one and the same theme in cosmic, social and individual contexts – in order to indicate that the sermon addresses our relationship to all of reality (see below ch.4).

Once again it should be stressed that the text and its interpretation have priority for the sermon. Rebellion against the primacy of the text is understandable if this is the text as controlled by official academic exegesis. But first, academic interpreters are not the administrators of the tradition but people with very different attitudes to their texts. And secondly, insights into the 'open text' have got through to most of them. Here primacy is being asked for this 'open text'. It is a text which constantly takes on new meanings in the context of life; part of a sign world which invites us constantly to make new contact with the ultimate reality through its images and narratives. Every sermon takes on a single direction through its task. It provides the basic theme for every sermon, which is played in infinite variations. So a separate chapter will be devoted to this theological dimension of preaching.

III

Preaching as an Opportunity to Enter into Dialogue with God: The Theological Dimension of Preaching

Only a century or two ago, everyday life and public life were steeped in talk about God, from God and to God. Religion was a public matter. That has changed. For many people, the few relics of civil religion are out-of-date references to a pre-modern period. The Enlightenment aim of making religion a private matter has been fulfilled today; indeed it has been surpassed in many spheres: religion and belief in God have changed from being a private matter into an intimate matter about which one speaks only with close friends. In many circles it is easier to talk about one's sexuality than about God.[1] All this has consequences for preaching. It becomes the only context for public talk of God – often even in the private human sphere. That gives it a particular task and responsibility. For people who go to hear a sermon are ready to open themselves to a voice which intervenes in an inner dialogue that otherwise is hidden: in an intimate dialogue with oneself which is carried on in the hope that God's word may 'join in'.

Any sermon lives on the hope of enabling contact to be made between God and human beings.[2] Without this hope it becomes random talk which could also be engaged in in other places, on other occasions, with another audience. Today more than ever the distinctive feature of preaching is that it is public discourse which speaker and hearers hope will make contact and dialogue with God possible. ('Private' discourse borne up by this hope would be part of a pastoral conversation.)

This central hope of entering into dialogue with God is grounded not only in the expectation of the hearers but in the religious sign system itself. For the distinctive feature of this sign language – in contrast to the sign language of art and science – is that it is completely governed by its relationship to the ultimate reality. However many other factors may in fact have an effect on it – its use as 'social cement' or as 'an aid to personal stability', and the tendency of traditions and institutions to maintain themselves – this sign language seeks ultimately to be more than an 'accompaniment' to human life dependent on such needs. It seeks to make human life possible as an answer and echo to God. The religious sign system strives for all elements of the sign system to be organized from this central concern. In pre-modern times it did this as a kind of metasystem embracing all the social part-systems: politics, economics, art and science. In modern times it partially competes with these autonomous part-systems.

Modern culture achieved its dynamic development among other things by organizing all spheres of culture by criteria immanent to them. It became so effective in economics because it coolly calculated everything in terms of profit and loss; science flourished because only the criteria of 'correct and false' were used and there was a rigorous priority of knowledge over all wishes and wants. Art flourished because it understood itself as a sphere of autonomous creation exclusively obligated to the criteria of what was or was not aesthetic. An autonomous principle of organization was discovered in all spheres of culture. The struggle for the autonomy of religion was embodied in the two greatest theologians of the modern world, Schleiermacher and Barth. Schleiermacher found the autonomous organizing principle of religion in an underivable human state, the feeling of absolute dependence. Barth, and with him dialectical theology, found it in the Word of God, understood as God's self-disclosure, as revelation.[3] Both approaches put forward the demand that in religion (or in faith) everything should be defined by its genuine 'subject', and that this 'determination' should run through all its statements. That is even more true of preaching. It aims at entering into dialogue with an ultimate reality, with God.

This aim of preaching can be formulated only as an opportunity and a hope.[4] For it evades purposive action, even if a sermon is directed towards this one goal and in so doing uses more or less 'appropriate' linguistic and intellectual 'means'. We can compare two forms of speech act which despite their unmistakable purpose can achieve their goal only by factors over which they have no control:[5]

1. First, all speech acts by which I appeal to the free will of others. This includes any real request and any declaration of love. However convincingly a declaration of love may be phrased, it cannot achieve its aim if it is not heard. Similarly, however well expressed and well thought

through a sermon may be, its effect depends on the will of its hearers, which is beyond the control of the preacher. No preachers *a priori* have a right for their voices to be admitted into those hidden rooms of the self where decisions on life are made. And no hearers have a guarantee of hearing God's voice in the words of a preacher.

2. Secondly, we might compare aesthetic language. There is no question that the whole work of the artist – style, language and ideas – has entered into it. Nevertheless, the success of a work of art is always the result of constellations beyond the artist's control. The work of a 'gifted artist' is 'grace' – although we know the tremendous amount of discipline there is in any work of art.[6]

Sermons come somewhere between declarations of love and works of art. They are speeches which can be planned, which do not succeed without disciplined work, but which can intend their success only in a broken way; for no method can bring about a dialogue between God and human beings. Sermons are what can be planned for an unplannable event.

So the special character of preaching is utterly bound up with 'God'. Its relationship to God defines the content and structure of preaching. And the difficulties of preaching begin from the fact that what we understand by 'God' has become ambivalent. So in a homiletical reflection, too, we must first of all talk about our understanding of God.

I now want to show how 'God' is present anonymously in human dialogue with oneself and others even in a secularized world.

The theological task of preaching then follows quite consistently. It seeks to make God present in the dialogue of human beings with themselves and others.

Finally, I shall discuss the consequences of this for the shaping of preaching, its imagery, inner tension and dialogue.

A. How does preaching seek to enter into dialogue? What do we mean by 'God'?

The place where we can most agree on what we want to understand by God in the modern world is the place of suffering. It is the place of theodicy, i.e. the attempt at a justification of God in the face of the evil of this world.[7] Suffering becomes the problem of suffering only if we think of two characteristics in the concept of God together: power and goodness, i.e. the expectation that God is powerful and that God is good. When Job complains that though he is righteous he has suffered so much misfortune; when the crucified Jesus cries out 'My God, my God, why have you forsaken me?'; when the modern age makes the innocent suffering of children an objection to God – it is always presupposed that God is both power and goodness. To put it in the words of the Catholic philosopher of religion R.Spaemann, whom I follow here:[8]

> In all these complaints, accusations and questions, two things are thought of together which in experience come together only some- times and by chance, namely that God is good and that God is powerful. And that God is essentially both. Were God only one of these two things, the complaint would make no sense. Were God only good, but impotent, then contrary facts could not be cited against God, since God could not change anything. Were God only powerful, but not good, then complaint would be meaningless because it would not find an ear. But in both cases it would be right not to speak of God. For nothing would be thought of in the concept of God which would not similarly be thinkable without this concept. It could be replaced by functional equivalents. God thought of only as power, as blind power, would only be an embodiment of facticity, an apologetic duplication and transfiguration of what is the case anyway and what we accept in resignation or punish with moral contempt depending on our inclination . . . God thought of only as meaning, as the impotent principle of good and not at the same time as the principle of facticity, of all being thus and not otherwise, would only be another word for a moral idea, an idea which arose with humanity and which will perish with it, at the latest as a victim of the increase of entropy in accordance with the second law of thermodynamics.

If we follow this explanation of the term, we have a criterion for appropriate talk of God: God is the unity of being and meaning, of reality and value, of power and goodness.[9] God is experienced negatively in the conflict of being and meaning; positively in the correspondence of being and meaning, in the fulfilled moments of life in which we can say 'All is well.'

I have used the terms 'meaning' and 'value' almost as synonyms.[10] However, one can distinguish between them. To find a 'meaning' in something is to experience it as if it contained a message relevant to our action and experience. What makes sense can be deciphered by our perceptive 'sense'. To discover a 'value' in something means to experience it as a possible goal of our willing and doing. What is valuable becomes the orientation of our decision and action. Value and meaning often coincide. We react to both with joy. We experience something as being in accord with our 'senses' and our will. We have the awareness that here is a resonance between us and surrounding reality.

Now all people learn valuable and meaningful things in their lives without necessarily perceiving the presence of God in them. A secularized consciousness and a religious consciousness interpret the same experiences in different ways. Wherein lies the difference? Two differences should be stressed: the character of response and the ultimate character of all experiences of meaning and value.

For an unreligious humanism, all value and meaning must be created by human beings. Human beings first bring the spark of meaning into a cold world. For only they can set goals, will aims, use and decipher material objects as signs. That is their uniqueness. By contrast, for a religious consciousness all the meaning and value which human beings create is a response and echo to an existing fullness of meaning and value. Human beings do not kindle the spark of meaning in a world which is free of meaning and value; it is kindled in them. The meaning and value that they create is a response to a meaning and value that they have received. All experience of meaning and value is first a response, an answer.[11]

Secondly, this given meaning and value has an ultimate character. For an unreligious humanism there can be only relative 'being' and relative 'meaning'. All the ultimate foundations of being and meaning must come to grief, as they end up in the trilemma of an infinite regression, a vicious circle or an arbitrary break in the process of reasoning.[12] Every value is a value only in relation to something else for which it is valuable. Every meaning becomes meaningful in a greater context of meaning. But these connections which we extend further and further somehow land up in a universe which is free of meaning and value. Similarly, every entity can be substantiated only by being put in a wider context which is either arbitrarily absolutized, or relativized in an infinite chain of wider contexts, or derived from whatever is to be substantiated by a circular argument.

By contrast, religious awareness responds to the spontaneous emergence of an ultimate unity of being and meaning: every entity in the world must be grounded in something else. But that does not apply to God. God is God's own ground – and the ground of all things. Any meaning and value points to something different; God does not. God is meaningful and valuable *per se*. God is a value *per se*. If human beings have intrinsic value and are their own ground, i.e. develop in freedom, then in this respect they are in the image of God.

The experience of God as an ultimate unity of being and meaning can be compared with human love. In the presence of the beloved all questions of value and meaning fall silent. They are answered. The world for the moment has a centre in the beloved, and anything connected with the beloved is good. The beloved is a value in himself or herself. When we are in love, we all feel the power to withstand even the greatest discrepancies between being and meaning in our lives, and to cope with them constructively.

As I have said, the experience of God is comparable. Faith is a kind of eroticism of being: in it the mysterious fact of existing becomes a miraculous event – something which is valuable and meaningful in itself. An infinite power to affirm being and living is activated: the self itself becomes the object of a will. It becomes a value in itself. It becomes a kind of message which says, 'It is good that you and all things exist.'

Anything that has an intrinsic meaning and foundation cannot be inferred from something else; it can only disclose itself, in disclosure situations in which we come up against something that has value, meaning and foundation in itself.[13] Such self-disclosure will always be experienced as the opening of a dialogue. For we only have analogous experiences with other human beings, whose authentic self remains hidden to us unless they reveal it to us themselves.

So the experience of God is the self-disclosure of an ultimately valid unity of being and meaning, reality and value. By it we are torn out of our everyday world, because in it we predominantly experience a tension between being and meaning. This happens in two forms, which can be understood with the help of the distinctions between indicative and imperative and between the hidden God and the revealed God.

In many spheres we attribute to ourselves the capacity to reduce or to preserve the unity of the tension between being and meaning through our action. Elsewhere our action fails us: here we can only hope for agreement between being and meaning. In the first instance, in the sphere of our responsibility, the unity of being and meaning is experienced as a 'message' in the form of an imperative, i.e. as a summons to realize or to sustain what is valuable. In the second instance, in the sphere beyond our responsibility, it becomes a 'message' in the indicative: even without our contribution, the valuable has always realized itself and will continue to realize itself. The religious experience of a unity of being and meaning thus influences life in two forms: as an indicative, 'being is good' (in which past and future are included), and as an imperative, 'the good should be' (in which the imperative comprises both singular and plural: no one stands alone in the face of this imperative).

But beyond the spheres of responsibility and trust there are dark areas in which both responsibility and trust come up against their limits: the sphere of unavoidable suffering which shatters our trust that there could be still some hidden meaning in it. The gulf between being and meaning seems to be final. That is the experience of the absence of God, the hidden God. Thus a decisive motif in the Christian tradition of faith proves to be constant recourse to the revealed God, the God who himself suffers in the suffering of his creatures, to the crucified Jesus who cries out, 'My God, my God, why have you forsaken me!' Christian faith is courage to live which is crucified time and again with Christ in order to be recreated *ex nihilo*.

Preaching has the task of opening up opportunities for a dialogue with God: a self-disclosing unity of being and meaning which is experienced in our lives as an indicative and an imperative, as a God who is hidden and revealed. It can fulfil its task by opening up experiences of being and meaning and making them possible: on the one hand experiences of discrepancy betwen being and meaning which offer the opportunity to enter into a dialogue of complaint and accusation, and on the other experiences of the consonance of being and meaning which are an occasion for thanks and praise.

B. The anonymous presence of God in human dialogue

I now want to claim that preaching can pick up an inner dialogue which we have with ourselves and with others, of a kind in which all human beings are always involved. It is often not a conscious dialogue with God, but God is anonymously present in it – as the question of the unity of being and meaning. The conflict of theodicy, between being and meaning, power and goodness, can also be experienced in secularized form: as a problem of the justification of the world, human beings and society.

1. The justification of the world (cosmodicy)

We are constantly occupied in gaining a meaning and a value for what is beyond our control. There is no problem with what we define through our action. For here we are ourselves the ones who give meaning to our actions. But what about everything that is independent of our action? This sphere that is beyond our control is not static space. Everything that sinks into the past from the present goes outside our control, even the action which we determine ourselves, in so far as it can no longer be changed. The only thing that we can change is our reaction to it. Whether and how we react, however, depends on whether or not we derive a kind of 'message' for our lives from it and what 'value' we discover in it.

A secularized consciousness will interpret the giving of meaning to what is beyond our control not as the detection of a hidden meaning but as a creative giving of meaning to what is intrinsically meaningless or meaning-free. A sickness or a handicap with which we must come to terms is thus interpreted as a 'test' of our courage. A new job or a new human relationship is accepted as a 'challenge' and a 'task'. But there is no one but ourselves who imposes the test here or gives us a task. However, precisely in this way we find ourselves in constant dialogue with ourselves, interpreting events beyond our control as gifts and tasks, trials and challenges. The decisive difference between the religious and the secular consciousness is that the religious consciousness accords metaphors like test, trial, challenge, gift and task a power to disclose reality. It is aware of the symbolic character of such statements, but is convinced that the metaphors point to something over against us which makes us look for meaning and value in all events that are beyond our control.

So we can say that religious faith gives meaning. It deciphers the world in the light of two basic metaphors for 'meaning'. Meaning occurs either as meaningful text or meaningful action. Religious faith interprets the world as if it were a text which one can read (at least in part); or as the expression of an action through which a value is realized. But what is true of all metaphors is also true here. They provide a stimulus for seeing reality in the light of them, but leave open how far the reality is what they promise. The only certain thing is that it is always also different.

Beyond doubt religious faith also attempts to decipher reality as a kind of 'text'. However, it is very well aware that no one can read the whole text. It is questionable whether it can be translated adequately into our language. At all events, human beings take part in constituting its meaning: it is an open text. The decisive thing for religious faith is to enter into a dialogue with God through fragments of this great 'text'.

Similarly, religious faith beyond question interprets all events as though they were expressions of an intention to act. But it knows that whether the values striven for by human beings will be realized is questionable. There is no 'plan' of salvation history which directs everything towards a goal; rather, everything is marked by human action, human responsibility and failure. Life is more a game in which the actions of the players are open. For religious faith it is decisive that human beings should interact with God by taking part in this game.

Religion gives meaning to what is beyond our control, by referring everything to God: the world is regarded as a text which God has written; history as a sequence of actions which God has brought about. But this claim also implies the inaccesibility of the meaning of the text as a whole, the fact that the whole meaning of the action is beyond our control. 'For my thoughts are not your thoughts, neither are your ways my ways, says the Lord. For as the heavens are higher than the earth, so are my ways higher than your ways and my thoughts than your thoughts' (Isa.55.8f).

Religion is the culture of an attitude to what is beyond our control[14] – beginning with the simple fact of our own existence and the existence of the whole world. It discovers in this existence a 'meaning', a message which means us – and a value, i.e. a goal for our behaviour, which gives orientation to our lives. We are always asking whether what happens contains a kind of 'message' (or a 'meaning'). We keep asking whether an event can be affirmed by us as though we had willed it ourselves.

2. *The justification of the self (egodicy)*

The internal dialogue of human beings centres above all on our own egodicy; we not only live but are constantly concerned to justify our lives – precisely where our own giving of meaning threatens to go off the rails and our behaviour offends against our own values. This inner dialogue is the experience of the 'conscience'.

The experience of the conscience has constantly deepened in the course of a long cultural evolution. Society in city cultures requires increasing human self-direction – and thus forms of moral behaviour which almost ask too much. In addition, modern individualistic culture confronts people with new imperatives for self-realization which on the one hand are signs of freedom and on the other a cause of anxiety about failing in the face of this new freedom. Finally, a specific modern challenge posed by the conscience to the self is that norms and values seem only to be relative entities. Depending on the context in which our individual action and will is put, it can appear as a heroic action or as a crime. But no one has control over the historical contexts in which his or her action comes to stand. In the end none of us can justify ourselves.

Paul already discovered the anonymous presence of God in the conflict of the conscience. He presupposes in all human beings an intensive inner dialogue consisting of accusations and defences, with the conscience as an incorruptible witness which shares in knowledge of our life. But in this inner process of judgment in Rom.2.14f. Paul leaves one role unoccupied: the role of judge, which God will occupy.

In fact we are always already confronted with God when in the conflict of the conscience we seek the unity of being and meaning, being and value in our own lives. In so doing, according to the religious self-understanding we follow a prearranged programme, namely the preservation of the image of God which is itself a unity of being and meaning. Of all creatures, human beings alone are the image of God, because only they struggle for this unity of being and meaning and only they doubt when it falls apart.

3. The justification of society (sociodicy)

All human beings are driven by the question of a unity of being and meaning at yet a third point: all societies justify the distribution of opportunities in life that have been established in them. In all of them we find an unfair division of power, possessions and education. In all of them there is a constant fight over distribution. It takes place between upper class and lower class, but also between peoples and societies. Premodern times attempted to use religious convictions to legitimate distributive structures which had become historical – and used the same religious convictions to protest against unjust distributive structures. Modern times have developed political systems of conviction which in some respects become the equivalent of religious convictions: capitalism, communism and fascism.

Why is there such pressure for legitimation on our social conditions? Why do people canvass for assent to distributive structures which have become historical? Is it simply because societies function smoothly if they are endorsed by those who live in them? Because they want to protect themselves against objections? Or is this pressure for justification grounded in the fact that every human being represents an intrinsic value which never simply represents value for others? All have the task of achieving a unity of being and meaning in life. But in that case everyone (as the image of God) has the same value, and that *de facto* we lead our lives at the expense of the life of others is a disturbing fact that we must either alter or justify. For it contradicts the conviction that all human beings are values in themselves.

God is also anonymously present in the social discussion of the legitimacy of the distribution of opportunities in life – in so far as each human being has his or her own value, represents an ultimate unity of being and meaning. That produces the great pressure towards justification to which all social systems submit. The constant fight for distribution of opportunities in life thus leads to the ideological legitimation of social conditions or to a constant 'sociodicy'.

To offer a provisional summary: God is the unity of being and meaning. Wherever people look for this unity, God is anonymously present: in the justification of the world, the self and society. In a secular consciousness, religious theodicy, i.e. the question of the unity of being and meaning, becomes cosmodicy, egodicy and sociodicy – in a constant dialogue with the self and others. Preaching means inserting oneself into this dialogue in order to become aware of the anonymous presence of God in it, in order to take up the dialogue with God. In this dialogue the questions keep changing. The decisive thing is that human beings do not have to justify the world, themselves and society by their thought and action. Preaching promises justification as a gift.

C. Preaching as an intervention of the Word of God in the human dialogue

If a sermon achieves its aim, it is like switching on a great light. One's own existence is experienced as 'message' and as value – with an intensity that we experience elsewhere only in a state of erotic love. We experience ourselves as 'meant', as 'willed' and as affirmed – not just something about us, but ourselves as a centre which is a value in itself. In preaching, it is not a human partner which provides this experience, but a power which underlies all being. The message is: 'it is good that you exist'. And it is good not only because it is good for this or that purpose, but because it is good in itself. And it is good because it not only means this or that person, but an authority which is independent of all human beings.

This message is communicated in the face of the deepest experiences of discrepancy: in the face of suffering and death, guilt and failure, injustice and oppression – i.e. in the face of the falling apart of being and meaning. The word of God is the illumination of the unity of being and meaning in our lives, contrary to the facts. It is the lighting up of God's present.

But how are we to imagine this present? God is not an object. Our own self is comparable. This self, too, never directly becomes the object of our contemplation and reflection. It can never look into itself completely – for that, it has to emerge from itself. It can only indwell itself in certain 'states'. And yet it is constantly present in our lives.

Usually this self is directed towards other things and persons, so that it is not even conscious of itself. But in particular situations of conflict and the great decisions of life in which this self struggles for its identity, it emerges from the background – not as one object among others but as a point of reference for all objects, which is not itself an object. God is also co-existence with all things and events in a comparable way. Only in particular disclosure situations does God emerge from his anonymous presence, so that we become aware of God.

These disclosure situations are either limit experiences in which being and meaning fall apart, in which case there is a consciousness of the absence of God. Or they are limit experiences in which the improbable correspondence between being and meaning is experienced as God's presence: in the beauty of nature or in the experience of trust and love.

The word of God is that human discourse which as such can provoke disclosure situations. It does not introduce any new object, 'God', into life, but brings out a background which is always already present. It makes contact possible with a reality that is not an object.

Here is an illustration of what it means that God is not an object. Discussions about the existence or non-existence of God often begin as if the concern was to distinguish between two great boxes of objects: on the one hand the mass of all the objects that exist, and on the other the mass of objects that do not. Generally speaking, mountains, trees, stones, but also toothaches, the number pi and the laws of physics are thought to exist. Things which are thought not to exist include the squared circle, the fiftieth moon round the earth, a society without conflicts, etc. One gets into difficulties simply in trying to sort things out.

This is even more the case if one wants to put 'God' into one of these boxes. God cannot be sorted into such boxes. For God is not one object existing alongside others but the box itself in which we meet all objects as existing. God is what decides whether something exists or not. God is the mystery of being. God is the framework of all things – but not a thing in this framework.

The word 'God' is justified only if this framework of all things and events that are not objective is experienced as meaning and value – i.e. as something which has meaning for our senses and value for our will.

If we keep to the picture I have chosen above, we can say that being is experienced as meaning where the 'box' becomes a frame which encloses a picture. The content of the picture may seem trivial, empty of meaning and insignificant – but as soon as an artist surrounds such an object, however trivial, with a frame, he or she is challenging us to seek a meaning in all that is trivial, empty of meaning and insignificant. God is like a modern artist. God communicates indirectly through a world which is full of the absurd, the ugly and the trivial. God is anonymously present in it. A religious faith senses that here something significant is making itself known. All preaching should open our eyes to seeing everything in a frame in which it is experienced as being significant.

But not only that: God is also a unity of being and value. To vary once again the picture with which we started: the boxes of being which we encounter in it can also be transformed into the frame of a stage, into the drama of the world in which we may see a role for ourselves, in order to take part as legitimate actors. The sermon should teach us to see reality as a drama in which we play a role for the shaping of which we are responsible and of whose value we are convinced.

So preaching becomes the word of God where it illuminates God as a unity of being and meaning. But how can that happen? Christian preaching relies on biblical texts constantly becoming the word of God for us, i.e. on there being a potential in them which so restructures our perception of reality that we perceive in it God's hidden presence or detect God's absence as loss and pain.

Here is an illustration of that. We all know the pictures which Gestalt psychologists use to demonstrate that our perception is an active process. By reversing figure and background in them we see now a goblet, and now two faces looking at each other; now an old woman, and now a young lady. Or in a confusion of lines we discover the hidden drawing of a person. Everything depends on how we structure and restructure the material – on the basis of anticipations which guide our perception. There is a wealth of such anticipations in the biblical texts: the basic motifs of biblical faith which allow us to discover something new in reality. In the light of the motif of wisdom, for example, we discover in a world which for many is just a conglomeration of particles and fields, built up on regularities which can be measured by mathematics, a superior reason of which our human understanding is just a weak echo. In the puzzle-picture of reality with its many confusing lines a power can be detected which addresses people, imposes an obligation on them and gives them security.[15]

If human beings are in constant dialogue with themselves and others in order to derive meaning and value from reality, preaching is a restructuring of this dialogue by incorporating God into it. Preaching becomes the word of God if it illuminates that unity of being and value which men and women seek, yet fail to find, i.e. if in reality it allows the experience of a hidden message and a value. The anonymous presence of God in the inner dialogue of human beings then becomes God's conscious presence. It is the foundation of the power to withstand the discrepancies of being and meaning that we endure – and of the obligation to reduce it where human action makes that possible.

D. Consequences for the shaping of preaching

Thus the aim of preaching is to make God present in the inner dialogue of human beings – as the unity of being which is not an object, which discloses itself in personal terms, but which cannot be inferred as something ultimately valid. The form of preaching is convincing only when it results from this aim of preaching. Four consequences for shaping sermons can be identified. First, preaching requires a specific *homiletical imagery*, because only discourse which employs images can fuse being and meaning and present what is not an object. Secondly, preaching calls for a *homiletical narrative structure*, because in this way the tensions between being and meaning, indicative and imperative, the hidden God and the revealed God, can be depicted without denying the aporias which remain. Thirdly, preaching calls for a specific *homiletical tension* which follows from the tension between being and meaning that runs through all our reflections. Fourthly, preaching calls for a *homiletical dialogue*; if the ultimate unity of being and meaning only results from self-disclosure, then one can only address this unity: one has to use an appellative towards it. Homiletical imagery, narrative structure, tension and dialogue thus follow from the task of preaching itself. I shall now go on to demonstrate this.

1. Homiletical imagery

A sermon without images and symbols will miss the mark. It is not just that images and symbols address people at the deepest levels, which abstract ideas find it hard to reach. Images and symbols are more than vehicles for a content which can be communicated even without them. Rather, their inner structure corresponds to the task of preaching on the basis of two characteristics:

(a) Pictorial language is discourse with open referents. Images are not only designations for something that is known but challenges to seek something unknown in the known. They are semantic disruptions which direct our attention to something new. A metaphor like 'house of being' says simultaneously both that being is a house and that it is not a house. What remains open is the degree to which being is a house. Those to whom the metaphor is addressed must and may find that out for themselves. The metaphor of the house of being certainly says something about the structure of being. It suggests that order, stability and improbability should be sought in it. It sends us on a search with an open outcome.

(b) Pictorial language is further characterized by a fusion of being and meaning. It includes both a semantic reference to a referent and a call to us to perceive a meaning and a value in it. If we sound out the meaning and value of reality, we are always making use of pictorial language. The metaphor of the house of being not only says something about ordered and stable structures of reality but also expresses their emotional quality and value. One may feel at home in a house. In a house one finds all one needs for living. A house gives security. But in it one also finds other inhabitants with whom one must get on, and not all of them are pleasant company.

Metaphors and symbols are beyond question particularly suited to pointing out aspects of reality which do not appear as objects and in which being and meaning emerge as a unity. Homiletically it is only possible to speak metaphorically of God as a unity of being and meaning who is not an object. So we should collect together, describe, develop all the images of God – and also invent new images, far beyond what a strict systematic theology regards as admissible. Homiletical images for God may be one-sided because they are effective only in an accumulation of images which supplement one another. God is sun and light, warmth and air. God is ethical energy and a magnetic field of meaning and value which pervades all of reality. God is the height and depth of being. God

is the heart of all things and the centre of the universe. He (or she) is the
total system of reality, the stream of life and the sea of being.[16]

However, the demand for homiletical picture language does not apply
only to talk of and about God. Any preaching has its place in an inner
dialogue about the world, the self and society. It needs images for talking
about these.

The whole cosmos can be covered in an image. Is the universe really a
'house of being'? Are we children of the cosmos – or are we gypsies in
the universe who have settled on a small planet as a tiny superficial
phenomenon? Or is the cosmos a giant wilderness on the edge of which
a tiny oasis flowers – our earth?[17] Such images for the universe often
contain an 'empty space' for God. If being is a 'house' – who is its
guardian? Who is the householder? If we are children of the cosmos –
what things in the whole system are 'fatherly' or 'motherly'?

It is the same with pictures which relate to individual life. Life, too, is
better grasped in images than by abstract ideas. Life is a great play – but
who writes it? Who enjoys it? It is a great voyage – but who is steering the
ship? It is a great examination – but who is marking it?[18]

And of course we also speak of society in images. Are we really a great
family? And isn't this family split by fraternal disputes – depicted by the
story of Cain and Abel? Isn't it like a great horde of apes in which
hierarchies are established by fighting? etc.[19]

Once again: images and symbols are not ornaments in a sermon.
They are part of its substance. The poverty of imagery in many sermons
is an offence against the task of preaching.

2. Homiletical narrative structure

Alongside images, stories are the most important means of preaching in
a vivid way.[20] No sermon should be without an image and a story.
However, a 'homiletical narrative structure' means more than narrative
examples or parables in sermons.[21] What is meant is a narrative
structure which follows from the substance of the sermon itself. All
biblical texts stand in one great narrative framework within the bipartite
canon of Old and New Testaments. The biblical narrative bears witness
to a history between God and human beings. The goal of the sermon is
to continue this dialogue. Here God encounters us in contradictions – in
the tension between being and meaning, indicative and imperative, as
the hidden and revealed God. We cannot solve these contradictions by a
theory which is free of contradiction, but must leave them side by side as

complementary statements.[22] A narrative description of such complementary statements is required by the facts because a narrative in
diachronic sequence can depict as a unity what is a direct contradiction
when taken synchronously and juxtaposed. Even if the sermon must get
involved in contradictions; even if it has to state that God is at the same
time hidden and open, immanent and transcendent, gracious and
powerful, personal and trans-personal, it will always start from
narratives in which hiddenness and revelation, transcendence and
immanence, power and goodness appear as consequences. The basic
structure of the biblical world of signs is narrative through and through.
In it the unavoidable contradictions of theological statements are done
away with.

I begin with the fundamental contradiction between being and
meaning. As early as the second century CE Marcion[23] found it so
central that he arrived at a belief in two gods: a god who was responsible
for the state of things as they are, the vindictive creator god of the Old
Testament, and the God of love and the gospel, through whom meaning
and value were first realized in a nonsensical world. Therefore the Old
Testament and New Testament writings could not possibly be part of
the same basic religious narrative for him. He therefore created a canon
consisting only of books of the New Testament – and adopted even this
only in a purified form from which everything that recalled the god of the
Old Testament had been deleted. Irenaeus of Lyons first gave a
convincing reply to Marcion with his theology of salvation history.[24] In
it, the contrast between creation and redemption was incorporated into
a comprehensive narrative. Redemption is understood as the restoration
and completion of creation after its fall. The creator God became the
redeemer by becoming man, so that human beings could fully realize
their image of God. A dramatic salvation-historical narrative depicted
how the original intention of creation is brought to completion despite
all resistance. In this way Irenaeus could integrate the complementary
relationship of being and meaning, creation and redemption, into a
narrative unity. He did not need to deny the tension between creation
and redemption. Rather, it became the basic motif of a narrative of
salvation history. In precisely that way he gave the bipartite canon of Old
and New Testaments a convincing theological basis.

In Protestantism, the tension between indicative and imperative is
often absolutized by means of the antithesis between law and gospel.
Protestants are fascinated by the idea that the Word of God works in an
inner sphere in human beings in which radical freedom prevails. There

the Word changes people so that they do good spontaneously without being guided by the law – as social control from outside, as the origin of internalized anxiety about judgment or as a command for the reborn. So Protestants sometimes dream of a radical anarchy of interiority,[25] i.e. of a lack of domination at the centre of human beings where the law no longer reaches. Consequently, for a long time in Protestantism the law could not be experienced as grace. Judaism was seen negatively as life under the law. The imperative was not heard in the indicative that was presupposed. This antithesis of law and gospel has been overtaken by a new sensitivity to narrative theology:[26] the liberation from Egypt precedes the lawgiving on Sinai as an indicative. The first lawgiving came to grief on human sin. The dance round the Golden Calf is a repudiation of the Decalogue. Nevertheless God renews his law. As a result of this, the law *a priori* becomes grace towards human beings who turn away from God. The lawgiving is an act of divine mercy. The basic narrative of Sinai can root the imperative in the indicative better than any abstract redefinitions of the relationship between law and gospel.

The tension between the hidden God and the revealed God can be worked out more appropriately in narrative form than by general theories: the story of Job, the Lamentations of Jeremiah and the Gethsemane narrative are better companions in the 'darkness of God' than any abstract theodicy.

Of course a theology must constantly sum up the wisdom contained in narratives in general statements and systematize it. It then arrives at complementary statements, and over and above that at a metatheory as to why such complementary statements are necessary.[27] However, general theological statements that are not tied to the narrative traditions of the Bible are open to misunderstanding. Only in the context of biblical narratives does it become clear that this creator God is at the same time the God of the exodus, who leads a people into freedom. It is the narrative context which first makes ambiguous theological statements clear.

3. Homiletical tension

There will probably be general agreement that a sermon should be gripping – simply because even those who listen to sermons with good will often suffer from boring ones. There are many legitimate means of achieving this. Thus one can tell a story and break off before the end, only taking it up again at the end of the sermon. Or one can deliberately touch on tabu subjects, so that the congregation holds its breath: surely he or she won't say such and such? (In political dictatorships even the slightest deviations from official ideology can activate the hearers.) Or one can disclose a piece of one's private life – and arouse the all-too-human curiosity to know something about the person in and behind the preacher. Or one can raise problems which make people ask, 'What's the answer to that?' All this is legitimate and often necessary. But these are not necessarily tensions which arise from the essence of the sermon.

The requirement for every sermon to be gripping is fulfilled properly where all the strategies which create tension are related to a basic tension, the tension between being and meaning. Both fall painfully apart in our experience. This split entangles people in an ongoing inner dialogue with themselves. A good sermon derives its intrinsic tension from this tension. Where the discrepancy between being and meaning is not evident down to the very depths, their unity cannot be understood as an improbable miracle either.

This requirement for a specifically homiletical tension does not mean that one must first conjure up the great discrepancy between being and meaning at the beginning of every sermon in order to show a way of coping with it – a unity of being and meaning from the Archimedian point. A sermon can certainly be constructed in this way. But it can also have another structure. One can also begin with a powerful statement of the experience of the unity of being and meaning – and then the abysses of life seem all the deeper. Indeed sometimes one ventures a look into the abyss only if one has a firm hold on the edge.

Nor is the demand for homiletical tension concerned with a symmetry between experiences of discrepancy and experiences of consonance, as though both had to be given equal importance – and possibly discussed at equal length. Often short keywords are enough to sketch out what moves and torments people in their inner dialogue. Often short sentences are enough to communicate the experience of a 'peace' beyond all reason. What is required, rather, is that the sermon should live by the tension which is provided by its subject-matter: the tension between being and meaning, reality and value, power and goodness.

This tension takes different forms. In respect of the past we are to think on the one hand of the suffering that we experience that is not our fault and to which we react with protest and complaint. But on the other hand we also need to think of the suffering that we cause by our own guilt – to others and to ourselves – and which leads to the request for forgiveness and renewal. The homiletical tension is destroyed if suffering experienced one-sidedly or guilt caused one-sidedly stands at the centre of all preaching.

This is repeated in respect of the future. Here our fears and anxieties are directed towards what is outside our control, however competent we feel about shaping the future. We are aware that the stream of time is taking us where we do not want to go: towards death. And we suffer this as the universal fate of every living creature (and as guilt only in the form of violent or unatoned-for death). But in respect of the future there is also an experience of the discrepancy between being and meaning which corresponds to the experience of guilt in the past: anxiety about failing in the face of the challenges which come upon us, regardless of whether this is collective failure (e.g. in the face of ecological crises) or individual failure in one's own scheme of life. In respect of the future, too, it is illegitimate to reduce the homiletical tension in a particular direction unless there is an expression both of the fear of future destiny caused from outside and the burden of responsibility where we ourselves can influence decisive factors.

But the real experience of discrepancy is that between being and meaning. We always live by experiences of a past meaning: of the trust of other people, of the adaptability of the world of the senses to our organs, the intelligible structure of the cosmos. And at individual points in life we keep experiencing intense moments in which we feel something to be a value in itself – above all in moments of erotic fascination, in a successful work or in deep understanding. All these experiences are symbolic of an ultimate unity of being and meaning which lasts beyond such fleeting moments: symbolic of God. So it is consistent for such experiences of a moment of self-value to be experienced by a religious consciousness as 'self-disclosures of God'.

At all events, it is the task of preaching to hold up against experiences of discrepancy betwen being and meaning a reliable experience of their unity. It seeks to illuminate this unity as a presence of God contrary to the facts. This illumination of a unity of being and meaning is initially a pure indicative:[28] those who have incurred guilt are promised that they are still accepted – despite guilt and failure. The sufferer is promised comfort, as a mobilization of all positive counter-experiences, but also as the promise of a paradoxical presence of God in suffering. Those who fear and are tormented with anxiety about failure are promised courage.

It would be impossible to resolve the basic homiletical tension between being and meaning had it not already been resolved in the basic Christian story – not so that it no longer exists, but in such a way that meaningful life with it is possible. The great questions of theodicy as they are still imprinted on the secularized consciousness in the ongoing justification of world, self and society are theoretically insoluble. They can be lived out in the discipleship of Jesus. If even God is exposed to suffering death, then this suffering and dying are no objection to an ultimate unity of being and meaning.[29] If God can be as present in the negative, absurd and painful as in the positive key experiences of life, then the covenant with God – a covenant with being itself – can also survive crises and catastrophes. There is no need to spell out here why and how christology represents an answer to the basic homiletical tension. It is enough to state that anyone who in preaching minimizes this basic tension, who brackets out the abysses of death, suffering and guilt, of injustice and oppression, will always see recourse to the basic Christian story of Jesus of Nazareth as an unmotivated 'christological' appendage and not as the centre in which the unity of being and meaning is permanently and reliably illuminated.[30]

4. Homiletical dialogue

Any sermon is an address to other men and women. Its basic structure is dialogical, even if it is presented as a monologue. In the framework of worship as a whole the sermon is built into a strongly ritualized dialogue consisting of hymn, prayer and creed. It is desirable for dialogical elements like laughter, clapping, murmuring to become customary again even during the sermon, to make it clear that a sermon seeks to open up a dialogue. That distinguishes it from a lecture which is entirely devoted to a subject and develops in accordance with intrinsic requirements. In a lecture, forms of address fade right into the background. The I-It relationship dominates. The virtue of the lecture is its matter-of-factness and its treatment of a subject, even if it contains a few dialogical elements. By contrast, in a sermon everything is related to an interpersonal relationship and ultimately everything is shaped as address, as a cry, a plea, a request. Everything aims at reaching the hearers, at opening them up, orientating them and changing them. That is even true of sections in which a problem is developed in a matter-of-fact way, for arguments and ideas, too, can open up people to a subject. However, in the end the sermon is address, call, appeal.

Here, too, it is crucial for this dialogical structure to emerge from the essence of preaching itself. For preaching seeks to be discourse which offers an opportunity to enter into dialogue with God. In the last resort it seeks to make it possible to address God and respond to God in personal terms.

Of course one can also give lectures about 'God'. In them one could perhaps make decisive statements about God, if we could infer an ultimate unity of being and meaning from the structures of the world, consciousness or society. If God could be disclosed in a logically stringent form, the philosophical lecture would be an appropriate way of making contact with God. But the state of our philosophy (or at least of my philosophy) is more that we can clarify the concept of God philosophically, including the fact that all inferences to God from the world, the self and society come to grief. But that means that philosophical reflection is concentrated on presenting the reasons for this failure – and in addition perhaps interpreting why people keep accepting it. The failure could in fact have heuristic value. It shows that the experience of God is an experience in which something is disclosed that in itself is foundation, meaning and value. It discloses itself in the same way as a person does in an encounter. Human beings ultimately disclose themselves through their own words.

If preaching is to be an opportunity of entering into dialogue with God, it must necessarily become address. It is comparable to a declaration of love, a request, a call, an appeal. That must also be expressed in its linguistic form. So at decisive points it will continually move from matter-of-fact accounts to direct address.

Many sermons suffer from having no imagery and no narrative structure, no inner tension and no element of address. But all these together would not achieve anything if they did not derive from the very essence of the sermon, making present an ultimate unity of being and meaning in the dialogue of human beings with themselves and others. Only in this way does preaching reactivate biblical sign language for the present. For in this sign language everything is orientated on a centre, on the central conviction that guides and organizes all basic biblical motifs, that permeates all images and narratives. This centre is belief in the one and only God. Wherever the sign language of faith is alive, it serves to make contact with God.

IV

Preaching as an Opportunity to Communicate an Orientation for Life: The Existential Dimension of Preaching

Any preaching enters into a dialogue about the world, society and personal life in order to make God present in it. It aims at an enhancement of life, i.e. to orientate and change life. In the New Testament the greatest enhancement is called 'eternal life'. John 17.3 gives the definition: 'This is eternal life, that they know you the only true God and Jesus Christ whom you have sent.' Here the enhancement of life is the presence of God in human life through the 'knowledge' of God – or, better, through the existential certainty of God. Three questions need to be raised:

A. How does such existential certainty come about?
B. How can it govern a whole life?
C. What consequences follow for shaping sermons and worship?

A. Existential certainty as an experience of correspondence

Old Protestant theology spoke of the internal testimony of the Holy Spirit, i.e. of underivable evidential experiences which cast light on the Word of God. In the framework of the theory of religion put forward here, we shall seek these evidential experiences in experiences of correspondence: in correspondence between the subjective basic motifs which guide our thought, experience and conduct and the objective structures of environing reality. I have called such experiences of correspondence 'experiences of resonance' and thus attempted to understand them by means of an aesthetic metaphor. It is as though a sounding board were responding to the vibration of a string, whose movements are amplified to become an audible tone.[1]

Such correspondence can arise in different ways. For example, we are certain of our basic motifs, sound out the varied fields of reality with them, and in so doing discover surprising correspondences. In this way the quest for 'wisdom' in the world keeps coming up against subtle 'wisdom structures' in objective reality. In the light of the exodus motif the whole natural history of humankind appears as an exodus from nature's house of slavery and human beings appear as the first free creatures. In the light of the motif of agape we perceive the varied forms of pro-social behaviour which first make life livable. In such moments life is harmonious for us. The basic motifs of our existence are confirmed. We have the intuitive certainty, 'Yes, it's like that. That's how life succeeds.'

However, the way to such evidential experiences can be different. We not only sound out various spheres of reality to see whether they correspond to our expectations and motifs but keep transforming our subjective motifs until they are 'adapted' to objective reality. We correct one-sided behavioural patterns and expectations, and often experience these corrections as a sudden disclosure. Evidential experience is based on the experience that the truth establishes itself in the face of our errors. Thus perhaps we have always sought 'wisdom' only in sym-metrical structures, in the harmonious and the successful, until it dawns on us that a hidden wisdom is also contained in the asymmetrical, the chaotic and the endangered. In such evidential experiences our previous basic motifs are not confirmed but expanded, transformed or replaced with new ones.

What is described here as a normal 'process of adaptation' is sometimes a far-reaching existential crisis. Religious certainty often develops in the experiencing and enduring of such a crisis. Often it is not enough for us to 'adapt' and modify existing basic motifs. Rather, they are completely shaken by impressions which contradict them: trust in them is lost. A whole 'world' collapses. The certainties by which we order reality *a priori* prove to be contingent and questionable. Here not only individual experiences are at risk but the condition of experience generally or the 'capacity for experience'. Here is the place where people come up against something that is not contained in their experience of the world but that first makes the world, themselves and experience of the world possible at all. This is the place where God is 'experienced'.[2]

Religious wisdom has always known that certainty is formed by the enduring of such limit experiences. In the collapse and rebuilding of an interpreted world a creative power is experienced – often as conversion, illumination, as being moved from the wilderness of darkness into light. What happens in such experiences of illumination and in evidential experiences is a reconstruction of the basic motives which guide our lives. The new takes the place of the old; the old is modified or given new intrinsic roots.

In any event, the presupposition for all evidential experiences is that we do not accept correspondences between subjective structures and objective reality as a matter of course. We must keep coming up against contradictions between ourselves and reality in order to be able to experience the correspondence that is discovered – whether through the disclosure of new spheres of reality or changes in our basic motives – as extraordinary and wonderful.

A sermon which seeks to bring to life the biblical sign language of faith on the one hand seeks to make it evident that reality continually discloses itself anew in the light of the familiar biblical basic motives: it seeks to confirm the basic convictions of biblical faith. On the other hand it seeks to root these basic biblical motives in human hearts so that they grow and mature there[3] – and this also includes their continual modification and correction, because subjective motives can never embrace the whole of reality. Here there is a metamotive behind all the individual basic motives, a central fundamental axiom: the expectation and hope that being and meaning, reality and value, power and goodness correspond in an ultimate reality.

B. The three dimensions of existential certainty

Now in what spheres of life do we find such existential certainty, i.e. evidence that the motives of our thought, experience and conduct that move our existence correspond with reality?

In my view, modern preaching is particularly one-sided in seeking such certainty primarily in personal life – in the sphere of interpersonal relationships. So-called existential interpretation has elevated this limitation into a programme.[4] According to it, the truth of biblical traditions cannot be found either in our understanding of the world or in our understanding of society: the 'world-view' of the biblical text is premodern and antiquated; the images and norms which governed past societies are out of date. The possible truth of biblical texts lies only in the human self-understanding. For it is the timeless task of all human beings in all ages to shape their own lives and to act accordingly. But understandings of the self, the world and society cannot be separated. Our understanding of ourselves is dependent on the place we give ourselves in the world and the way in which we think about history and society. Existentialist interpretation itself is an example of this. Its relationship to the world and society is predominantly negative; for it, nature is the sphere of determined freedom, society the sphere of an inauthentic 'they' (i.e. a pre-formed role relationship). An opposition is postulated between nature and society on the one hand and true personal existence on the other. Authentic existence is conceivable only as a radical inner distancing from nature and society. Here human self-understanding is related to an understanding of the world and society with a markedly negative colouring, indeed is dependent on it.

Once again it must be emphasized that we are in a constant dialogue with ourselves and others about the world, society and the self.[5] Accordingly, preaching has the task of not just intervening in the dialogue about human self-understanding but being present in all the dimensions of this ongoing dialogue. Nowadays the cosmic dimension of preaching is usually neglected. So I shall begin with it, and then go on to discuss the social and personal dimensions. All three dimensions together form the existential dimension of preaching.

1. The cosmic dimension of biblical sign language

Religious sign systems have always had the task of assigning human beings a place in the universe – alongside things, plants and animals. They have an 'ecological function'. To some degree they listen in on nature for a hidden message which has two aspects: an indicative statement about the place of human beings in the cosmos and an imperative instruction about their task of preserving, caring for or developing this cosmos. Now in the modern world, religion has lost control of the picture of the world.[6] The natural sciences are responsible for what is the case (indicatively). They fall silent when it is a question of evaluating the place of human beings in the cosmos, i.e. establishing whether it is a meaningful or meaningless place. The imperative aspect, that of showing human beings their place in the cosmos, is even more beyond them. They say nothing about the human task. Some thinkers stamped by the natural sciences even explicitly dispute that there could be an imperative for human beings. They must formulate their own imperatives in an indifferent world.

The danger of preaching and theology is that in this situation it either goes back to a premodern metaphysic and holistic interpretation of the world in order to formulate that unity of 'is' and 'ought' which has been lost to the modern consciousness or that it forgoes cosmic statements so as not to create tension with the modern understanding of the world. In the latter case the quest for the unity of being and meaning, reality and value, is abandoned. There is a limitation to meaning and duty. Statements about creation are transformed into an ethic of creation.

Or are there 'bridges' which enable us with a good intellectual conscience to give a religious interpretation of nature and to incorporate the cosmos into our sermons? May we understand both as the text and history of God without lapsing into premodern naivety?

I have chosen a parable to illustrate the contribution of semiotics to this problem.[7] Imagine that we are cast on a desert island – either through shipwreck or in the course of an expedition. The island seems to be wild and uninhabited. We go into the interior. There we discover on the ground a regular triangle made of stones. We immediately recognize that it is a sign. So we say: behind that there is the intention of communicating something or asking for something. 2. We are not alone on the island. Other intelligent living beings must be there – people. The presupposition is that we have found a configuration of normal things which as such is improbable and simple, and which stands out from a less ordered background by virtue of this simplicity and improbability. We experience such a pattern as a challenge to give it a 'meaning', i.e. interpret it as a pointer to something else. Suppose that an intelligent being like a rat also went past the triangle. I have chosen the rat as an example because psychological experiments today have convinced us that there is a certain image of the rat in human beings. This rat sees the same stones, but cannot interpret them as a sign. At best one could train the rat by 'classic conditioning' to regard the triangle sign as a signal prompting a particular form of behaviour, e.g. a quest for food, by regularly putting bacon on stone triangles.

Thus the parable. Now its theological meaning. We all come into this world as if on to a strange island. We do not know whether we are alone in this giant cosmos. But as they go through the world, some sensitive people are struck by 'signs', improbable configurations of normal things, patterns. Indeed, these people experience the whole world as a sign and simile of something else: God. They suspect that they are not alone in this world. A superior, incomprehensible 'intelligence' is at work in it. Everything is a sign which points to it. Others see the same constellations but do not experience them as signs.

Beyond all conflicts of interpretation between these people, one thing is certain. All signs are based on patterns of physical or biological signifiers without being identical with them. They are comparable to a melody (i.e. an acoustic pattern). The melody remains the same regardless of whether it is played on a piano or sung by a child, whether it is high or low, whether it is audible or only written in notation. Patterns are not identical with their natural vehicles. The same pattern can be realized through different vehicles. Now it is beyond dispute that the world is full of such patterns. But that does not indicate their significance. Rather, meaning is attached to patterns by people, just as we put a text to a melody. There is a wealth of texts that one can sing to the same melody. But not all are possible (simply because of their length) – and not all are appropriate. There is no necessary connection between patterns and their significance, with the exception of iconic signs, in which there must be a relationship between patterns and what is depicted. So we find a connection between vehicles, patterns and meanings. There is a continuity between them, but no necessary relationship: the same pattern can be realized through different signifiers, the same significance through different patterns.[8]

Religious interpretations relate to the existing pattern in nature and the cosmos. Their existence is indisputable. What specific interpretation can be attached to them is open – as is whether one deciphers an existing meaning or creates one, whether one finds meaning or produces meaning. Nature is like a melody to which we attach very different texts. But there is no dispute that one can attach such texts. There is no disputing the possibility of interpreting the pattern. For some it is perhaps just 'poetry' in which human emotion is expressed, but for others it is 'sacred poetry' which points to God. However, it is improbable that we are projecting on to a world which rejects all meaning.

The natural sciences are telling us more and more about this pattern. Above all they show in the framework of evolutionary thought that the whole of evolution consists in a constant increase and differentiation of patterns. One of the most complex structures of patterns known to us is the human brain – with the capacity to recognize patterns and attach significance to them. The natural sciences relate something like a powerful epic: the epic of evolution from which human beings have emerged. They show that human beings are not just genetically pre-programmed, are not just shaped by their environment, but – like any system – have the capacity to direct. They are a self-organizing system, and they are also aware of the fact. They feel responsible for their action and for the success of their existence. This epic basic structure of our knowledge makes nature (within an evolutionary framework) accessible to a religious sign language. For it, too, has a basic epic or narrative structure. Both the epic of evolution and the religious myths of cosmogenesis cover the origin of the human race.

So what is related in scientific language as the epic of evolution can become a part and parable of an epic of creation. It can become a parable for God (the disclosure of a hidden unity of being and meaning) in the light of the basic biblical motives. With their help connections are discovered throughout evolution which make it possible to put ourselves in the cosmos and define our task without having to refer back to illusory interpretations of totality. The result is not holistic systems but regionally limited fields of evidence in an enigmatic cosmos. The great paradigm of such a theology is still the thought of Teilhard de Chardin, even if we cannot continue his pre-modern evolutionism (which counted on teleological factors and led to an overall system).[9]

I would like to illustrate what I mean with a couple of examples. In the light of the motif of creation we keep having an intense experience of the contingency of things. Time becomes a profound riddle, the present a transition between the 'not yet' of the future and the 'no longer' of the past. Because everything is contingent, there is no immediately illuminating ultimate evidence: the contingent can only be noted, not confirmed.

Today we experience nature in the light of the motif of wisdom overwhelmingly as 'rational'. Generations before us would never have dreamed of discovering as many new connections and improbabilities as we have. The ever more complex patterns which are grasped in space and time allow us to read the 'book of nature' with increasing fascination.

Finally, we experience nature in the light of the exodus motif. All life is an attempt at adapting to reality. But only human beings are conscious of this as a task. Only they can take their fate (and their task) into their own hands. Today even the threads of evolution on our planet have been put into our hands. A tremendous task awaits the first free creatures.

Because the biblical sign system, like any other religious sign language, once fulfilled the objective task of showing human beings their place in the cosmos, I am arguing for an evolutionary hermeneutic of the Bible for the present.[10] Biblical religion, too, is part of a great process of trial and error through which living beings develop structures of adaptation to the world. Here human beings have a special task. They know that the world that they experience is only an environment specific to them – and is different from objective reality. They face the task of developing structures of adaptation to a reality which transcends their world (their limited niche) and for which they therefore have no 'natural' organs. In my view, religion is the specifically human form of adaptation to such an ultimate reality. Here biblical religion is an attempt to seek a new correspondence to this ultimate reality by changing human beings. Above all it contains the great insight that all human attempts at adaptation ultimately come to grief. No human being succeeds in making his or her life correspond to God. Everyone fails here. However, at the centre of biblical religion is the certainty that this ultimate reality nevertheless accepts all these failing variants of life – *sola gratia, sola fide, sine lege* – and that this certainty is communicated through the one man Jesus.

The wisdom which is hidden in our and other religious traditions has probably not yet been fully recognized. Everywhere life developed structures of adaptation long before there was an awareness of the fact – far less a recognition of how and why such structures were 'adapted'. An evolutionary hermeneutic begins from such a 'wisdom of adaptation' contained in the religious sign systems – and of course can later conceptualize it. It is part of faith in search of knowledge: *fides quaerens intellectum.*

2. *The social dimension of biblical sign language*

Religious sign systems have always had the task of co-ordinating human action and making co-operation possible despite the constant struggle over the distribution of opportunities of life. Here, too, we find an indicative and an imperative function of religious language and imagery side by side. On the one hand they legitimate what is. They put the often so questionable aura of holiness over existing circumstances. Here the issue is not the indicative which states what is but an evaluative indicative which recognizes that the given is valuable. At the same time religion provides an orientation on what is to be – often as a protest against what exists and is valid at a given time. The indicative of value is supplemented by the imperative of what should be.

Here too modern awareness has led to a deep change. The legitimating function of religious sign language is suspected of being an ideology. For example Paul's conviction that all authority is appointed by

God (Rom.13.1ff.) is an unwieldy piece of tradition. Religion is suspect if it seeks to make given circumstances acceptable. By contrast, the imperative function of religion looks different: where there are stimuli towards love, justice and freedom it is accepted – at least as an ally, even if it is an inconvenient ally for modern contemporaries. Its prophetic solemnity exposes it to the suspicion that it is not capable of pluralism. The unconditional seems to break open the argumentative discourse of a secularized society.

The correct insight here is that modern theology and preaching are threatened by the danger of a social-ethical moralism – regardless of whether this moralism makes conservative or progressive gestures. For in a modern society even a Christian conservatism is no longer the quiet prescription of the existing ethos. On the contrary, in the face of secularization it becomes a radical critique of society. The implementation of the morality that it inculcates would be a conservative revolution – and precisely for that reason it is not conservatism in the classical sense. Both variants of a social-ethical moralism lack a balance between the indicative of a recognition of reality (i.e. of the values which are always already realized in it) and the imperative of protest and change. But this very balance is contained in the religious traditions: 'ought' is grounded in a status or a being. Those who are confronted with an imperative are first promised a value by a promise in the indicative.

The question is not whether only the protest element of religion (whether formulated in a conservative or in a progressive way) is legitimate, but what we may already recognize as a value before any 'ought'. To open eyes to this is a central task of religious sign language. Here we should accept and regard as a gain the fact that the aura of holiness which once surrounded the most important social institutions has been destroyed. We should be sceptical about attempts to restore it artificially. For only human beings are holy and unassailable. All institutions should serve them. This is not so far from Paul when he denies the state and the authorities a direct religious legitimation (the emperor is no god), but grants it an ethical legitimation: it is to promote God and resist evil – and in so doing be a 'servant of God for you' (Rom.13.1ff.). But that only becomes clear if we read what Paul says as an alternative to a much wider religious legitimation of the state (i.e. as an alternative to the emperor cult).

The dignity and value of human beings – those are the things given by the indicative which even theology and preaching can only discover. They cannot create them. They cannot even formulate them as 'oughts'.

They can only attempt to open people's eyes to them. And here they could create tension with modern society. For in the meantime tendencies have developed in it to remove the aura of holiness from individuals as well. That becomes particuarly clear from the fact that there are those who are prepared to withdraw from the unborn that unconditional right to life which can be put in question only in a tragic conflict with a competing right to life. It becomes clear in the fact that comparable uncertainties can be detected in the attitude to the old and infirm. The insight that human beings have a value – independently of their achievements and their contribution to the whole of society – is fading. But this very conviction must be maintained among those who cannot 'contribute' anything because of an emergency, in the case of the old and sick and also refugees and foreigners.

Every human being is the image of God. All human beings have a value in themselves which may never become a means to another end. A sermon which is certain of this always also has a political function. It limits the fight over the distribution of opportunities for life.[11]

But how can preaching escape the barrenness of moral imperatives? How can it avoid the dictatorship of a scheme of society presented with prophetic solemnity? How can it remain free from sterile radical conservatism? How can it provide orientation in the social sphere – and in so doing remain capable of pluralism, i.e. show respect for the various political tendencies in the community and in society?

Here, too, the memory is important that we do not have our ethical traditions as a system of modes of action or as a scheme for society, but as a narrative tradition in which the complexes of commandments are embedded. The Bible contains a narrative ethic.[12] It does not just formulate norms but shows in narratives what the indicative presuppositions of these norms are (e.g. God's covenant, the gift of the land, the image of God in human beings), and it shows how human beings deal with these norms, come to grief over them. It shows how they become models for further behaviour – models which one can follow without having to imitate. The narrative form of biblical ethics is liberation from the dictatorship of moral imperatives.

Christian social ethics are related to the biblical tradition as the development of a story that has already begun – a task which we often give children in school. We test whether they have grasped the normative genres and the decisive motifs of a narrative by giving them only the beginning of a story and asking them to provide a continuation. Here there are always several possible continuations. But there are also impossible conclusions. One cannot end a love story like a ghost story; that would offend against the norms of the genre. But within the norms of this genre there is room for a legitimate pluralism of continuations and conclusions. It is the same with the biblical story. It is not yet finished. It is our task to complete it. The norms of the genre by which we examine the legitimacy of our rival continuations are those basic biblical motifs which I attempted to describe above. We apply them consciously or unconsciously in order to judge whether or not a particular action is Christian. But they allow different 'continuations'.

We do not need any finished ethical system in order to apply such basic convictions. Here are some examples. The conviction that every human being has a chance to alter his or her behaviour changes our attitude to criminal actions, and actions which deviate from the norm. People can change. Anyone who denies that drops out of the biblical consensus. The motif of a change of position, the motif of agape, relativizes the fundamental social limits between above and below, between insider and outsider. These basic motifs change attitudes both to hierarchies and to the members of alien groups and nations. The motif of self-stigmatization contains the conviction that a message can be contained in suffering. In the light of this we shall have to ask time and again what message the stigmatized in our society are expressing. It is the task of preaching to emphasize such basic motifs. Preaching may and should discuss concrete conclusions – but always with the proviso that this is the preacher's conclusion. It is possible for others in the community to come to different conclusions.

In order to make biblical texts fruitful for the future, it is important to distinguish between recurrent basic motifs and variable concrete norms. An informed sociological exegesis helps here.[13] It can liberate from absolutizing biblical norms. It can show how the basic biblical motifs have developed in history, how they are made effective or compromised in particular situations. It measures ethical statements by the historical possibilities of human actions. For example, in our day we cannot renew the lists of household rules from earliest Christianity as a valid morality. But a historically informed exegesis can draw attention to interesting features. Thus it is taken quite for granted in I Peter 3.1–6 that a wife may differ from her husband in religion. Here earliest Christianity, too, did not recognize the husband's authority. In Eph.5.25ff. Christ is presented as a model of the husband's behaviour. The point of comparison is not his rule but his self-surrender. Here the husband takes on a role which tends to be assigned more to the wife; even in antiquity, sacrifice for the husband was also regarded as a virtue of the wife. Here it is required of the husband. We recognize such features only when we look at ethical statements in their historical framework.

Sociological hermeneutics here makes it clear that all the texts of the Bible stand in a social framework of action, even if we can no longer recognize this as clearly as we would like. The discovery of this social dimension of the texts is more important than any individual results. If it is an inalienable element of the exegetical consciousness that all texts are conditioned by social factors and in turn have functions in social contexts, then the social conscience is already sharpened by being occupied with the biblical text: the reactualization of biblical sign language has even more of a social function in preaching. Preachers have a social responsibility for it. They can perceive it all the better, the clearer they are about the social function of biblical sign language and texts in the past.

3. The personal dimension of biblical sign language

Biblical sign langugage is above all an opportunity for men and women to enter into dialogue with God. Only the individual can start on this dialogue. No one else can conclude a covenant with being in his or her place – a covenant in which human beings respond to an overwhelming unity of being and meaning with a 'Yes' to life and to all being. This 'Yes' is also promised for the future. It is also a promise of loyalty for times of crisis.

Faith here becomes the basis of human identity – a correspondence of human beings with themselves despite all biographical breaks, despite tensions with their environment, despite contradictions between what ought to be done and what is done in their own lives. Such identity has two aspects. First, it is identity which is given. We do not seek who we are. We do not choose either our parents, or the time and place of our birth, or our bodies with their limitations. Secondly, identity is a task. It is realized by our following a scheme for life for the realization (and conception) of which we have a large measure of responsibility. Thus personal identity must 'achieve' two things: coping with contingency and self-fulfilment. On the one hand this is a matter of coping with everything that we already face on our way to self-fulfilment, everything that limits this and even thwarts it: experiences of injustice and suffering, the limitations of time of life, competence, health, having one's own irreversible past catch up on one. On the other hand it is a question of self-development and self-fulfilment – despite all these limits, often against them, often even in a transcending of contingent factors which is thought impossible. It is certainly the case that all of us can become happy only within our possibilities and not beyond them; however, it is not *a priori* certain what these possibilities are. No one knows precisely.

Because of this two-sidedness of identity, here, too, preaching also has the task of finding a balance between indicative and imperative. Indicatively it accepts identity as a gift: it recalls life as the gift of the creator and promises new life as the gift of the redeemer: as 'new creation' in the midst of this world. At the same time preaching formulates an imperative: the imperative of responsibility for one's own life and its realization within a limited human life.

The danger to present-day preaching is that it often deals with contingency in a one-sided way – comfort in the limit situations of life – or one-sidedly aims at self-fulfilment. The former certainly corresponds to an objective function of religion which has proved to be incapable of being secularized despite all enlightenment and secularization:[14] the more we hope to achieve a just distribution of the opportunities in life through our action, the more bitter and irrational is their ineradicable inequality: the unequal distribution of health, gifts and beauty, the arbitrary blow of 'accident statistics' to an individual life full of hope, the arbitrariness of happiness and unhappiness. However, particularly among young theologians this objective function of religion that is undoubtedly present is set against another awareness: for them, faith and religion are often primarily motive forces towards a self-fulfilment that deviates from current schemes of life in a secularized society. The central theme then becomes transcending the boundaries of life rather than coping with them – especially where traditional patterns of life with historically conditioned and changeable limits must be abandoned (for example in the role of women). That preaching and faith also make it possible to 'accept fate' is often (and rightly) suspected of being a misuse of religion.

This tension recurs in hermeneutical concern about the Bible. For Drewermann's depth-psychological exegesis of biblical texts, all biblical symbols and images become an expression of the quest of the self for itself.[15] The central symbol 'Christ' is regarded as a symbol of the self, his way as a way towards self-fulfilment. Self-fulfilment presupposes that one frees oneself from the fetters of limiting anxiety. Here the psychological function of biblical texts is seen above all as one of reducing anxiety.

This interpretation of biblical texts, which to my mind is one-sided but which finds a great response in the present, should be a challenge towards developing better psychological exegesis. It is certain that religious texts have power to give a basis to (and challenge) identity. But the question is how one can make responsible statements about them which can be tested by the texts and do not contain any illusory assumptions about human identity.

Both Drewermann's exegetical method and his implicit anthropology (or psychology) are to be criticized. For him, the texts are the starting point for a rediscovery of the return of a timeless picture language (the language of the images of archetypes and universal symbols). He does not interpret the concrete biblical texts, but the timeless imagery beyond these texts, which he postulates and already knows in advance. The method of amplification taken over from Jung makes possible a random association of related images and symbols with the text. It legitimizes a detachment from concrete texts.

His psychology is equally one-sided. It has no understanding of the functions of institutions in removing burdens, of the involvement of human beings in historical and political situations. Anxiety is not timeless, but specific to each situation. But above all, religious sign language not only has the anthropological function of liberation from anxiety but also aims at making anxiety possible. It seeks to motivate people deliberately to expose themselves to anxiety – to the anxiety of death, e.g. when it speaks of the possibility of martyrdom.[16]

There is no room here to sketch out a more appropriate form of psychological exegesis.[17] At all events, the narrative character of the biblical tradition will play an important role in it. Identity is formed through history – and in the capacity to present one's own history in stories that are narrated. If we want to say anything about what we really are, we will tell our life stories. These individual histories are open to wider stories. It makes a great difference whether we set them primarily in the history of the nation or in the history of God with human beings which is attested in biblical religion. In such overarching stories we find the models for identity, and for coping with anxiety and conflict.[18]

Christian identity is formed by our finding models for our lives in a history from Adam and Eve to Paul (from Justin the apologist to Dietrich Bonhoeffer).[19] All the models remain external as long as we do not internalize the basic motifs which are at work in the narratives of these models. Identity is formed in connection with the Bible by letting these motifs guide our behaviour and experience so that reality is constantly disclosed afresh in the light of them.

We can make a provisional summary: in all three dimensions of the existential orientation of life, preaching is concerned to find a balance between indicative and imperative. This task is identical with the task of making God present in all existential dimensions. For God is the dynamic union of indicative and imperative, of being and meaning, reality and value. Where this unity lights up in our lives, God is present. So if biblical sign language is to be reactualized in preaching in order to make it possible to enter into dialogue with God and orientate our life in all its dimensions, we shall read biblical texts not with the help of a uniform hermeneutics but side by side in the light of an evolutionary, sociological and psychological hermeneutics. Each is one-sided in itself. Even together they do not produce a whole which is without contradiction and tension. But practised side by side (and expanded by further approaches to the Bible) they help us to bring our lives more into line with God – in search of religious truth and existential certainty.

Here is an outline which sums up these results and gives a survey of the dimensions and functions of preaching that we have discussed.

	Indicative Attributes value	Imperative Indicates action	
Cosmic dimension	Shows place in cosmos	Indicates task in cosmos	Evolutionary hermeneutics
Social dimension	Legitimation of the intangible	Imperative of the changeable	Sociological hermeneutics
Personal dimension	Coping with contingency	Self-fulfilment	Psychological hermeneutics

Dynamic unity of
being and meaning
reality and value

The dangers of modern theology and preaching can easily be identified from this sketch. Often a dimension is absolutized. M.Welker speaks of three Babylonian captivities of present-day theology: a holistic metaphysic, social moralism and a dialogistic personalism.[20] No form of theological thought can claim to represent the whole. Furthermore, the dynamic unity of being and meaning is lacking from all three dimensions – whether in a conservative or a progresive rigorism. The enhancement of life and existential truth are found only where human beings correspond to God in all dimensions of life as a dynamic unity of being and meaning, reality and value, indicative and imperative. Preaching seeks to convey such an enhancement of life.

C. Consequences for the shaping of preaching

But can any sermon be formulated which does justice to these demands? Isn't it too much to ask of concrete preaching that it should bring about existential certainty in all dimensions of human life – in our relation to the cosmos, to society and ourselves? Isn't too much expected of preaching if it is to intervene in the inner dialogue of human beings with themselves? Aren't sermons expected here which are far more extensive (in their thematic breadth) and intensive (in their existential significance) than real preaching can usually be?

1. Multi-dimensional preaching

One of the best-tested rules for preparing sermons is to concentrate on one point but to make this clear and impressive. Treat only one theme. But how does that relate to the three-dimensionality of preaching called for here? Doesn't such an aim lead to an extensive overloading of the sermon? Indeed, priorities must be chosen. In my view, in normal circumstances there seems to be one clear priority: as a rule the personal dimension has priority for the individual sermon. Here, briefly, are some reasons why.

Addressing the individual has priority because the lifetime of the individual is limited. The universe and society will survive the individual. But the individual might perhaps be dead before the next Sunday. And even if the individual's situation is not so dramatic, after all he or she is now in church – perhaps after long inner hesitation – to make another attempt at 'God'. Perhaps the sermon has a unique opportunity. Perhaps someone has come who is deeply depressed, for whom everything is just too much. Is such a person to go home without an offer of renewing the covenant with life? Surely one must attempt to bring some clarity to a person's life? In every sermon I attempt to tell myself that there could be someone among the congregation who is preparing for imminent death. There could be someone making a last attempt to enter into dialogue with God. There could be someone desperately struggling with suicidal fantasies. All of us have limited time. There is perhaps a unique chance to reach someone. Hence the priority of the personal dimension in preaching. Personal problems are always topical.

Similarly, there are situations in which the social dimension has priority for preaching. Time and again there are crisis situations in the life of a society to which an answer must be given now and not later. In these situations, for most hearers the personal and social dimensions of life become fused. Here the social theme must be given priority. But it is important for the foundations for such themes to have been laid in previous sermons. In times of crisis one is referred back to what was worked out in more peaceful times. This work is always meaningful. For general social questions are always topical as the background of our personal lives, even if they only sometimes emerge directly in them.

Only the cosmic dimension is to some degree timeless, apart from those times when nature breaks into the human world in catastrophes. In that case the place of human beings in the universe also becomes 'topical' – and then too, unless foundations have been laid previously for dealing with this cosmic dimension, they cannot be laid first in times of crisis.

From these reflections one might draw the conclusion that there was a clear hierarchy of priorities. At all events, utterly personal promises and claims have priority. Only then follow the social and cosmic dimensions of faith – in that order. So it should be emphasized that this may be taken as a rule for individual sermons. But for preaching generally it might even be necessary to give priority to the cosmic dimension. Why?

In modern society human beings increasingly live in special worlds, each with its own norms and values and each with features which are taken for granted. The functional differentiation of society leads to very different sub-cultures. And often quite different individual forms of life can develop within such sub-cultures. All statements about the whole of life are thus under suspicion of coming from the limited perspective of a social or individual special world. That makes it all the more important to remember that all these special worlds exist within one and the same cosmic framework. We are all 'children of the cosmos'. We are all affected by the ecological crisis. Here we all face the same challenge.

Hence the demand – regardless of the need for every sermon to address the individual – to elucidate the whole of human existence in all its dimensions in preaching. This three-dimensional character of preaching can be achieved quite simply without asking too much of the individual sermon:

1: by setting the individual sermon in a cycle;
2: by the liturgical framework of the sermon;
3: by concentrated images in the sermon.

Here are some reflections on that.

(a) Setting the individual sermon in a cycle

No sermon is the first, and none is the last. That relieves one of having to say everything that is important for faith in one sermon. The normal course of sermons and readings in the church's year helps to balance out one-sidedness. Deliberately planned series of sermons can make people even more aware of this inner cohesion of different themes.

(b) The liturgical framework of the sermon

I noted above that the personal, social and cosmic dimensions can take on various degrees of topicality. Similarly, they can be connected with various genres in worship. By its form the sermon is the part in which one can most easily move to topical questions. The more timeless a theme, the more it can also be taken up in the recurrent framework of the liturgy (in which the variation is only slight).

It is already striking in the Bible that cosmic themes appear above all in hymns. Heaven and earth, nature in its beauty and strangeness, are relatively timeless subjects. Descriptive praise refers to them. In the New Testament Jesus Christ is praised in hymns as the mediator of creation. In worship, hymns and songs would also be an excellent place for meditating on the place of human beings in the cosmos. But where this cosmos becomes a topical issue in the present – as in the ecological crisis – it can be addressed in the confession of sin. For we are ourselves ultimately responsible for the present drastic reduction in the variety of organic life forms, for the emigration of birds, for defacing creation.

Intercessions form a constantly recurring context for the social theme. As an example, here is an intercession which I keep using with slight variations. It should speak for itself.

Our God,
we pray for our world.

For the churches in it,
that they may represent the gospel credibly.

For politicians and governments,
that they may solve conflicts without violence,
in the Balkans, in the Middle East, in South Africa and elsewhere.

For society,
that it may produce goods for all,
including those in the East and South.

For schools and universities,
that they may serve truth and people throughout the world.

For nature,
that we may see it as your creation
and preserve it throughout the universe.

We pray for all those who are weary and heavy-laden,
for the sick and dying,
for addicts and those at risk of suicide,
for the divorced and for mourners,
for the handicapped and the lonely,
for refugees and those seeking asylum,
for prisoners and the neglected,
for all the losers in our society.
Let us help to ensure
that they are not lost.
For Jesus Christ's sake,
Amen.

(c) Concentrated images in the sermon

However, the demand for three-dimensional preaching can also be
fulfilled within one and the same sermon without the addition of three
sermons which would have better been given one after the other. The
decisive thing is to succeed in bringing alive one and the same image in

all three dimensions, thus providing three variations on one and the same idea. One should attempt such sermons, not always, but now and again.

The image of the 'wilderness' in Luke 4.1ff. might serve as an example.[21] According to my definition this is a symbol. For the wilderness is on the one hand a real landscape in Palestine and Syria, while on the other, as an image it has surplus meaning which one cannot exhaust in one and the same sermon. The wilderness is the place of liberation from Egypt, and in it lies the mountain of God – the place of the giving of the law. But the scapegoat is also driven into the wilderness on the Day of Atonement to bear the sins of the people there. So the wilderness is also a place of the uncanny, that which is hostile to God, and a place of death. I was able to use only a small part of these dense symbolic meanings in a sermon on Luke 4.1ff. However, in our context it is decisive that the image of the wilderness is varied in a threefold way.

(a) First of all the wilderness is interpreted as a symbol of the universe as a whole. For in our eyes the universe is uninhabited, although in it – as in the wilderness – more hidden life could be contained than appears at first sight. At any rate the whole of human culture is just a small 'oasis' of life in the lifeless cosmos. The first basic existential decision consists in saying 'Yes' to this questionable oasis of life, although it is threatened. We are expected to be partisan on behalf of life.

(b) In the second part of the sermon the wilderness becomes the symbol for the limits of society – for those spheres of life which escape normal society. They make possible a much sharper criticism of it. From the outside perspective of the 'wilderness' the one-sided distribution of oportunities in life seems deeply problematical. The second basic decision that we are required to make is therefore to say 'Yes' to the weaker ones in the struggle over the distribution of opportunities in life, to offer partisan support for life which is threatened in our human culture – support for those who do not get their due and the losers in our society.

(c) The third part of the sermon makes the image of the wilderness transparent to the personal existential dimension: the wilderness is the place of renewal. In the middle of it John the Baptist issues a summons to conversion. This renewal is never achieved by those who are not prepared to go into the inner wildernesses of their lives, where the unrealized possibilities of their own lives lie: the life that is not lived, all that is destroyed and violated in life. Therefore the third basic decision is a 'Yes' to the questionable life in ourselves, to what is weakened and threatened in every individual human being.

God has come to human beings where they offer this partisan support for threatened and endangered life; where it becomes important for them to be recruited by God on behalf of endangered life, to commit themselves like God to their own endangering and weakness; and where the certainty is alive that God in person takes the side of weak and questionable life – within the universe, within human society and within the personal life of individuals.

I shall add variations on a second image, and then I can draw a general conclusion.

The narrative of the exodus from Egypt is clearly tied to a particular context: to liberation from political and social conditions which cause suffering. Interpretations which do not bring out this social dimension will not do justice to the biblical texts. Nevertheless the image of the exodus can also illuminate the other dimensions of human life. I have already pointed out that cultural evolution is a great exodus from the limits of biological evolution. Human beings are the first free creatures. The same image in turn can be applied to processes of liberation in personal life: any 'exodus' from neurotic compulsions and anxieties is a dramatic event – also with a longing to go back to 'Egypt'. It, too, has crises like the crossing of the Sea of Reeds: the powers of the old life once again prove to be frightening forces. This is the way in which Drewermann has interpreted the exodus.[22]

If one regards such 'variations in imagery' as legitimate, one is presupposing that there are processes in different dimensions of life which are akin in their formal structure. Wherever life establishes itself in the face of a hostile environment, there is a comparable constellation of factors. Wherever liberation takes place, there are typical processes. So images have the power to elucidate in different dimensions, even if originally they are only at home in one of them. If you like, this leads to a (homiletical) rehabilitation of the kind of allegory which once expressed the biblical tradition in the Middle Ages and which kept relating it to the present.[23]

2. Preaching which produces cognitive restructuring

A sermon becomes existentially significant if it intervenes in the inner dialogue of men and women with themselves about the world, society and their own lives. This is not just an 'extensive' problem for preaching, of how it is to address the whole of reality, but also an 'intensive' problem: how can preaching reach the point where decisions are made about life? How can it be a constructive influence on inner dialogue in men and women? And how can it do this while respecting the 'intimate spiritual sphere' to which every human being has a claim?

First of all it can be objected that a sermon is the wrong place for such intensive 'interventions'. How can public discourse have such a personal effect in a ritual framework? That is something for pastoral conversation or therapy.[24]

Here, too, in my view, the opportunities for preaching are underestimated. Precisely because of the distance from the everyday world which the ritual framework provides, there is an opportunity to have a constructive influence on it. One could make this clear by a comparison with a therapeutic conversation. Here, too, there is a 'ritual' framework. The conversation is limited to between fifty and fifty-five minutes, although the problems addressed could take up very much more time. Here too detachment from the everyday world is sought: one cannot both enter into a therapeutic relationship and have a teacher-pupil relationship or an authoritative relationship to the client at the same time. But above all, the therapeutic relationship is helpful because the reactions of the therapist are not everyday ones. First there is a chance to work through much that is dysfunctional in everyday life. It goes without saying that therapy can and will achieve far more personal change than a sermon.

But how can the sermon have existential and personal effects? It can give powerful stimuli to individual hearers to see their lives differently: to live them more attentively, to assess some things otherwise, to revise attributions of causes. In short, the sermon can provide stimuli towards cognitive restructuring, so that those who hear it comment on their lives in a different way. It has this opportunity by virtue of its central content, the relationship to God. Its message is: from God's perspective everything looks different – including your life. Here too this message is brought closer by images and narratives than by abstract notions.

(a) Images as means of cognitive restructuring

As is well known, one can comment differently on a half-full glass by saying either 'It is half empty' or 'It is half full'. And that is true of much in life. The half-full glass is a prime example of cognitive restructuring with the help of an image. The pessimist sees only the empty glass, the optimist the full one. But both are right. The sermon on Mark 13.31–37 in Chapter VI contains an example of cognitive restructuring in a sermon by means of an image. Its theme is given by the church's year, the overcoming of mourning and loss; and its central image by the text, the image of the house whose inhabitants are waiting for the return of the master of the house. In this sermon the mourning of the disciples over the death of Jesus becomes the model for mourning generally. Its phases of anger against the dead person, against God and against oneself, are played through one after the other. The image of the abandoned house expresses the situation of mourning. Now a cognitive restructuring is achieved with the help of the imagery of the house: the abandoned house becomes the house waiting for the return of the master, in which the inhabitants want to live together in the spirit of the master of the house. The associations of the abandoned house are replaced by new associations: a house is also a home and a space to live in. The move towards life, the activating of competences – all that is now faithfully bound up closely with the one who is absent. The admonition of the text, 'Watch', is translated in terms of the situation of mourning by 'Live attentively'. Depression and mourning cease where we again register life intensely, note differences and pay attention to our surroundings.

(b) Narratives as means of cognitive restructuring

One important way of seeing one's own life differently is to regard it from the perspective of someone else. We can gain distance from ourselves by asking, 'What would X say to your problem?' Or, 'What would you say if a good friend came to you with this problem?' The change of perspective is 'therapeutic' in itself. This can also be encouraged by the retelling of stories from another perspective. One example is the retelling of Acts 10 from the perspective of the 'stinking' tanner Simon, with whom the great apostle is living.[25] This tanner has a social stigma – his appalling smell. One could begin from the fact that in most communities there are people who like Simon the Tanner seem inferior and socially isolated, though in the eyes of many people the defect which isolates them is not so great a problem. Even without the sermon saying so directly, the hearer senses that there are different ways of dealing with such social stigmas. Here the narrative becomes more vivid and effective than any direct appeal.

At the end of this discussion I should stress that not only can individual images and narratives achieve cognitive restructuring; that is also the aim of the central content of the Christian message. The inner dialogue of human beings aims at the justification of the world, society and life. But the message of the gospel aims at the justification of a person. If a person is *simul justus et peccator*, then he or she learns in every act of worship to have a different view and pass a different judgment: the righteous as sinner, the sinner as righteous; the impotent as powerful, the powerful as powerless, and so on. Justification is a cognitive restructuring made possible by the word of God which leads to a change in life.[26] Acceptance of the self without deception is beyond doubt the aim of many sermons. Because God recognizes human beings unconditionally, they are encouraged in a relaxed way to perceive their strengths and weaknesses and deal with them. Whether this message ever goes home is another matter. The preacher does not have sole control over this. But the preacher is responsible for seeing that the message is not distorted from the start and that the message of justification does not degenerate into the sorry lament, 'So God wants an excuse for the existence of such a poor and wretched person as me!' The result of that is that the 'good news' is heard, but it makes the hearers sad.[27]

V

Preaching as an Opportunity for Communication between Preacher and Community: The Communicative Dimension of Preaching

In every sermon, preacher and congregation enter into a relationship with each other. Here criteria applying to any communication apply. Preaching has rightly been investigated by means of general communications theory and psychology; communicative styles have been distinguished and normative criteria for successful communication worked out. In the first section I shall sketch out some results of communication studies which in my view are helpful for the analysis and preparation of sermons. The consequences for shaping sermons which follow are orientated on the ethical criteria developed in communicative ethics. Here special emphasis will be placed on one value which is decisive for dealing with the substance of preaching: orientation on the truth. A whole section is devoted to it.

A. The four levels of communication

The starting point for all communication studies and the psychology of communication is the distinction between content and reference in any act of communication. We can follow F.Schulz von Thun in differentiating the referential aspect further into three levels.[1] The 'sender' of a communication always gives away something of himself or herself in speaking – often without words, through intonation, gestures and other non-semantic circumstances relating to the expression. To this degree every communication has a level of 'self-communication'. At the same time speakers (implicitly or explicitly) sketch a picture of their relationship with those who are being addressed. Any act of communication therefore also takes place at a referential level in the narrower sense. Finally, every communication (implicitly or explicitly) contains an appeal to the recipients, even if it is just an appeal for them to understand it. But often more is expected: conclusions, actions, changes of attitude. Together with the level of the subject we thus arrive at the following square of communication:

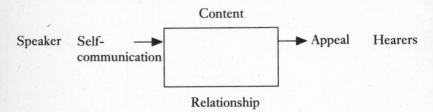

To give an example. The comment 'The window has now been open long enough' not only contains the content 'A window is open' but implicitly the message 'I'm cold', and an appeal to shut the window. Something quite certainly emerges from the overall situation about the *relationship* between speaker and audience: the speaker could be in a position in which he or she expects someone else to shut the window as a result of what is said.

Communication succeeds only when it succeeds at every level of the communicative act. Therefore there are norms of behaviour for every level. Together, they form a communicative ethic which makes clear to us how we should behave if we are concerned to communicate successfully. So in what follows, a normative value will be described from each of the four levels of communication.

F.Schulz von Thun[2] has shown that the norms of successful communication are best described as a balance between two polar values – and as a contrast to contrary values (or non-values) which follow from exaggerations of communicative values. That may sound abstract, but the first example should make it clear enough.

1. *Comprehensibility*. The first condition of successful communication is that the *content* communicated should be understandable – a balance between lucidity or unequivocal clarity and allusive ambiguity,[3] i.e. the capacity to allow overtones and undercurrents which enrich any

objective information. The contrary value to unequivocal clarity would be obscurity – a blurred form of discourse to which not only theologians are prone. A contrary value to allusive ambiguity would be trivial simplicity: here everything is arranged in a pedantic or meaningless way. No undertow of interpretation is detectable. A telephone directory is trivial and clear in this sense. One can regard it as a drama with an extremely long cast list and an extremely brief action. All in all we arrive at the following 'value square' for comprehensibility:

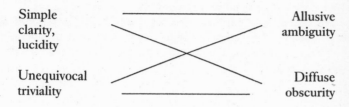

Simple clarity, lucidity   Allusive ambiguity

Unequivocal triviality   Diffuse obscurity

2. *Authenticity*. In so far as every communication contains some communication of the self, we expect it to be authentic: speakers should stand behind what they convey. They should say what they think. But here, too, we move between two poles. On the one hand is a consistent truthfulness which includes the capacity to convey one's attitudes, opinions and feelings even where they may not be wanted. On the other hand there is a deliberate personal style, extending to the effect of what is said. Such a style is also authentic. For it has grown up with us in a long life: beyond question it is part of us. Those who think they see an inauthentic façade here are missing real life. The contrary value to a style conscious of its effect would be a (misplaced) bluntness, and the contrary value to truthfulness an inauthentic façade. That gives us the following value square:

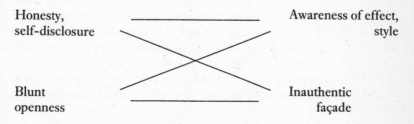

Honesty, self-disclosure   Awareness of effect, style

Blunt openness   Inauthentic façade

3. *Respect for fellow men and women.* Any communication says something explicitly or implicitly about the relationship between the speaker and the audience. We expect the communication to be made with respect. And here, too, we move between two poles which constantly need to be rebalanced, between proximity and distance. On the one hand we value it when someone accepts a conversation partner and shows empathy. On the other hand, we expect tact and courtesy, i.e. a distance which makes a confrontation over unpleasant matters possible without causing hurt. The contrary value to such tact, shown with sympathetic respect, is a false courtesy[4] in which all conflicts are stilled. Real life has departed from it. We experience a harmonious façade. The counter-value to empathy and acceptance would be the aggressive disparagement of the other. That leads to the following value square:

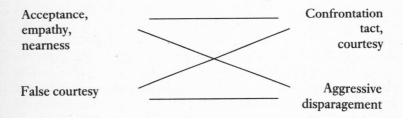

Acceptance,   Confrontation
empathy,   tact,
nearness   courtesy

False courtesy   Aggressive
                                                          disparagement

4. *Responsibility.* Any communicative act contains an appeal, and an attitude of expectation from the audience. The expectation can also be of an 'inward' attitude, understanding, thought, interpretation, etc. At any rate, any communicative act seeks an effect. In one-sided communication in particular the responsibility of speakers increases. They have rhetorical power. They are responsible for the effect of their words on their audience. For they can misuse their power. Such reponsibility is always a matter of balancing out two values: on the one hand a desirable competence to guide and provide orientation, and on the other a liberality which leaves hearers freedom and deliberately limits the power of the speaker. The contrary value to such liberality would be demagogy, i.e. the use of every possible art of rhetorical persuasion, also for dubious ends. The contrary value to competence in guidance and orientation would be a disinterested *laissez faire*. The value square would then look like this:

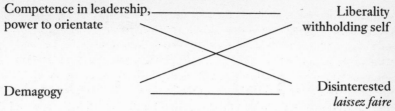

Competence in leadership, power to orientate — Liberality withholding self

Demagogy — Disinterested *laissez faire*

The four communicative values of comprehensibility, authenticity, respect and responsibility largely have parallels in the values of a communicative ethic. Following Habermas, one can formulate four conditions in which communication is also successful in preaching.[5] The language must be comprehensible. The statements must be honest. The conversation partners must have respect for each other, i.e. respect each other's traditions, convictions and values, even if they do not share them. Finally a common concern for the truth is presupposed, i.e. a readiness to submit to objective criteria. This last point is missing from the list so far. In my view it is so central that it must be discussed as a separate aspect. It relates to the level of communication, but has consequences for every aspect of the levels of relationship. Therefore the responsibility of the speaker is absent – understandably – from Habermas' communicative ethic. For the problem of this responsibility becomes acute only where there is an exercise of power and domination with words. A communicative ethic orientated on a dialogue free of domination aims precisely at avoiding such an exercise of power. In this respect it does not correspond to life as it is actually lived, but to an idea on which this life is in fact orientated.

Communication comes about in a variety of ways. There is not just one style of communication. Empirical studies of sermons have succeeded in distinguishing two basic types of sermons: sermons in a personal dialogue style and sermons in the style of dogmatic testimony.[6] It is not difficult to fit these two styles of communication into our square. The preaching style of dogmatic testimony is orientated on the convictions and norms of Christian faith, whereas the personal dialogical style involves the introduction of the person of the preacher and deliberately makes use of the preacher's relationships to the community:

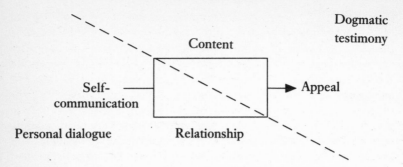

One could make a further differentiation with the help of four types of
preachers. This has been formulated following F.Riemann:[7]
A.Denecke has described them as the profound preacher of knowledge,
the responsible preacher of order, the changeable preacher of freedom
and the sensitive preacher of love.[8] Certainly these are only ideal types,
but they can cover a manifold and complex reality. The preacher of
knowledge concentrates almost automatically on the level of content,
the preacher of order sees the texts as a responsible structuring of the
'levels of call', the preacher of freedom introduces subjectivity into the
communication most freely, even to a degree going beyond traditional
norms. And the preacher of love is concerned for empathy and intimacy.

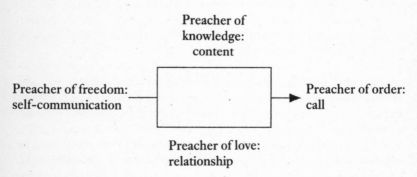

Certainly, yet other typologies of communication styles and the
corresponding personality profiles could be sketched out. F.Schulz von
Thun distinguishes no less than eight styles of communication:[9] the
assertive, the selfless, the aggressively disparaging, the demonstrative,

the defining and controlling, the detached and the dramatic styles. However one may distinguish and differentiate, everyone is governed (usually unconsciously) by the premises of such communication styles, i.e. by personal axioms of experience and behaviour. For example, the selfless live by the spiritual axiom 'I myself am unworthy – I can be of use only in commitment to you and to others.'[10] The aggressively disparaging follow the spiritual axiom 'There's something wrong with me, I can get anything right. What a disaster if anyone notices. Then I shall be scorned and depised mercilessly.'[11] Preachers are human beings like everyone else. They have their destructive and constructive spiritual axioms. They are all obliged, in their own interests, to overcome the one-sidednesses of their inner 'programming'. An intense preoccupation with the world of biblical signs can be of help here. If we take this world into our innermost self in profound meditation, we can let its 'axioms' work on us – in, with and under the old spiritual axioms of our life. For example, the selfless may learn (not only with the head, but in a way that permeates their whole lives), 'I am an infinitely valuable creature of God.' And the aggressively disparaging may learn, 'I'm all right, and my mistakes won't destroy me.' Only by allowing the conscious and unconscious motives of their own lives to be intensely steeped in the basic biblical motifs will preachers become credible witnesses, not least by letting the tensions which arise from encounter with the biblical world of faith work themselves out in their persons.

B. Consequences for the shaping of preaching

Preaching is a one-sided form of communication. But it is a section of a more comprehensive conversation which the preacher is having with the community. Some preaching is a reaction to a conversation that the preacher has had before; some conversation in the community is a reaction to a sermon. Nevertheless, preaching is a one-sided form of communication. It is unavoidable that it should be criticized as an authoritarian form of speaking. Despite this criticism, dialogue sermons have failed to become established. They have remained an exception. On the contrary, preaching as a monologue has been able to maintain its place, and there are good reasons for this – on all four levels of communication:

(a) *Content.* We always give a knowledgable person the opportunity to express his or her thoughts in a connected and careful way. That is possible only in a longer discourse. And democracy does not live just by a culture of discussion but by the art of public speech. Without speeches, public discourse becomes superficial. Without sermons, theological reflection in the church would also become superficial.

(b) *The appellative side of communication.*[12] A public speech which is not followed by discussion to some degree gives individuals greater freedom to define their own nearness to or detachment from the subject-matter than a conversation. For in a conversation individuals are always called upon to adopt a position and say what they think. In particular those who are at some distance from the church therefore prefer to listen to a sermon rather than to enter into a direct conversation.

(c) *The level of reference.* Here, too, the sermon has not only defects but particular opportunities. In any discussion group differences emerge: differences in attitude to the subject-matter or to persons. In the sermon, in principle all are equally near to, and far from, the subject-matter and the preacher. To some degree the sermon is more 'egalitarian' in so far as preachers do not put themselves above the community by an exaggerated sense of office.

(d) *The expressive side.* Here, too, the sermon has a special opportunity. Self-communication and self-disclosure can both hurt. No one has complete control of the course of a conversation. The greater spontaneity of self-disclosure in a conversation therefore has its limitations.

Even if the sermon is one-sided communication, all the criteria of a communicative ethic apply to it: comprehensibility, authenticity, respect, responsibility, and a concern for truth. However, these criteria must be spelt out with reference to preaching.

1. Comprehensibility. A sermon is a public speech given within a limited period of time, but in an unlimited cycle of other sermons. A sermon is rhetorically appropriate if in this situation what it says is understood and comes home. That calls for more than just clear language. There is a need to gain the hearers' attention successfully, to respect the limits of their attentiveness, and to direct their attention towards the decisive points, and so on. All this serves for comprehensibility in the framework of a lengthy public speech.

2. Subjective authenticity. Preachers must not only mean honestly what they say and say what they mean. They are judged on whether their life matches what they preach from the pulpit, or whether they can convincingly deal with discrepancies between message and life.

3. Respect for fellow men and women. One can persuade hearers of

something only if one takes their norms, values and traditions seriously – particularly where one wants to contradict them. Certainly there are limits: preachers cannot and and must not give the impression of accepting what in reality they reject as being the prejudices of their hearers. If they do, they lose their credibility. But in any event a programmatic contempt for one's hearers (as in some branches of dialectical theology) would be an offence against communicative ethics.

4. Responsibility. All preachers share responsibility for the consequences of their words, in so far as these words derive from their actions and are not influenced by circumstances which prevail against the best intentions. It is inappropriate to delegate responsibility for the consequences of a sermon completely to the 'Holy Spirit' or – in resigned variants – to the 'unholy spirit' of the time, which robs the best words of their effect. However, one can take responsibility only where one has a realistic picture of one's possible influence. Therefore empirical studies of sermons are very important for the ethic of the preacher. They clarify what preachers can achieve. But they do not cover all the effects of sermons.

5. Concern for the truth of the matter. No one gets anywhere with an audience who is obviously concerned solely with getting over to them. Credibility derives from concentrating on a subject to whose criteria one submits. Sermons are to be measured by a general sense of truth and a Christian sense of truth. Here the decisive factor in any verdict on a sermon is not how near to or far away from objective truth it is, but what its intentions of the truth are.

No relationship between these five criteria is free of tension. There can be substantial problems which cannot be given appropriate rhetorical treatment in a space of between fifteen and twenty minutes. Subjective authenticity and respect for fellow men and women affect the identity of preachers and hearers. It is a matter of the self-respect of the preacher and his or her respect for others. Both can be in tension if, for example, a liberal theologian has to preach to a congregation with a fundamentalist stamp (or, conversely, a fundamentalist theologian has to preach to a liberal congregation). In such circumstances can preachers really say what they think without provoking irritations? For the sake of tact and respect are they to keep quiet on those points where they differ and where they will cause offence?

In discussing individual criteria, we must reflect that the problems addressed can never be subjected to one criterion – otherwise there would be no possible tensions between them.

1. Comprehensibility

The following reflections are merely marginal notes on a topic which deserves more thorough investigation. The aim is comprehensibility, including its most basic presupposition, the attention of the hearer. 'Incomprehensiblity' in preaching (and not just there) is a serious offence against a communicative ethic. But how are comprehensible sermons to be achieved? What is to be said about sermons which are both lucid and full of those overtones that convey more than what is actually said?

The style of speech must be mentioned first. Sermons should go at a restful pace, with possibly a more rapid tempo for stylistic deviation. We need pauses to let sentences and words make their effect. We can listen more easily when the tone generates dynamics and liveliness, preventing monotony. But above all, sermons should not just be read out. The sermon is not there for the manuscript but the manuscript for the sermon. It is good to see a manuscript there. That tells us that the preacher is prepared. But it is even better if we forget the presence of the manuscript, if the sermon seems to rise again new from the pulpit, newly thought through, newly formulated – all while the preacher is looking at us. Then we are certain that the preacher is not making a prepared statement, but is really speaking to us, to those who are actually present.[13] Although one can practise and learn such free speech, one rarely comes across it. Usually sermons are read out. Here the speech can rapidly become written speech, i.e. speech which is basically addressed to those who are not present.

If one asks those who listen to sermons about their ideas of an appropriate way of speaking, one immediately provokes protests against special ways of speaking in church: against the patriarchal language of Canaan, against modern pastoral jargon, against the fog of academic formulae. And rightly so. Nevertheless, the call for everyday language in preaching is one-sided and even misleading.[14] For any good style consists in measured deviations from normal language. It is only the too frequent and repeated deviations from it that we feel to be mannerisms; only the conventionalized deviations that we feel to be jargon; only deviations that are inaccessible to outsiders that we feel to be elitist. However, we enjoy minor deviations, from the slight alienation of everyday language which makes us see familiar words in a new light, through the unaccustomed use of traditional biblical language in new contexts, to humorous word-play on familiar jargon. So it would be wrong to put particular words on a list of bad words. A word cannot be stylistically good or bad in itself, only its usage. So there are no tabus for the language of sermons, though it is necessary for all deviations from the normal language of a particular community to be measured: they are to be experienced as deviations within common language and not as a departure into another language – into the language of Canaan, the language of administrative Christianity or of academic profundity. The language of preaching will always differ a little from everyday language. It should combine lucidity and ambiguity. For we must make our everyday awareness transparent to the wholly other in order to make contact with God. The language of preaching will always be a particular dialect – or, to be more precise, a 'sociolect'. If we wanted to exclude all the elements of this dialect, we would also have to dispense with words like 'God', 'grace,' 'forgiveness', 'repentance' and so on. But that is impossible. The language of preaching may be a particular 'dialect', but it must be a 'dialect' within the language that is generally used. It should be a living 'dialect', not a historical one.

A further condition for the comprehensiblity of a sermon is that it should be possible to follow its structure.[15] It is not a matter here of having a refined structural pattern of the kind that can be discovered only by academic analyses, but of constructing the sermon so as to hold the attention. A sermon must itself ensure that the central statement is emphasized. It must end up in a point. It should be a unity. Many sermons that I have heard were really a mixture of three sermons. One creates unity by indicating a theme and by the recurrence of the same images, phrases and leitmotifs. One can shape the conclusions of individual parts like a refrain. However, no unity should be so perfect that the sermon is predictable. Rather, the art lies in arousing expectations – and correcting them in retrospect where they have been fulfilled. Here, too, the principle of measured deviation from what the hearers expect applies. And here, too, such 'measured deviations' create that balance between unequivocal clarity and allusive ambiguity which fascinates us.

Expectations are aroused, among other things, by formal divisions. A dry 'first, secondly, thirdly' is quite inappropriate. Links are needed. For example, one can divide a sermon on the motif of 'the wilderness' into three imaginary excursions into the wilderness. Or one can question three experts on a problem. Or ask about the three most important things one would take to a desert island.[16] Or relate the three most outrageous things that one has experienced in the church. It is not the number but the division which is to hold the attention and arouse expectations.

Anyone who arouses expectations must fulfil them in the course of the sermon. If this is done convincingly, the sermon will have an organic conclusion. It will indicate a return to the image used at the beginning, the question posed initially, the use of a concentration of different imagery in the sermon to make its point once again. This should not be a summary. On the contrary, it is a good thing for even the final rounding off of the sermon to contain a measured deviation from the argument so far: a point, a small surprising phrase.

I have often already touched indirectly on a further criterion for comprehensibility: vividness. No preacher should restrict what is said to abstract ideas, however correct they may be and however human the intention. What a twenty-minute talk leaves in the memory is principally images and narratives or narrative fragments. So it is a good rule of thumb that no sermon should lack images or narratives. But elements of imagery and narrative do not in themselves guarantee success. Both must be integrated into the argument of the sermon. Think of how many forced stories anyone who has heard sermons must have listened to, stories which either have not been evaluated at all or which point in a different direction from the ideas of the sermon. How many images remain mere ornament! Yet every image has a value of its own which points beyond its rhetorical function. In successful imagery clarity and ambiguity are combined.

Finally, one more thing that is desirable: a sermon should be a form of address which leads to an inter-personal relationship. It seeks to be promise, encouragement, invitation, consolation.

2. *Subjective authenticity*

It is often said with a solemn Protestant concern for honesty that preachers should say only what they think. They should bear witness only to what they live out in their lives. And beyond question, as we listen, we can tell whether a sermon has a setting in the life of the preacher or whether it is merely tradition that is handed on. But it is hard to say how we detect this.

Do we detect the speaker's involvement in the form of language used? Do we sense that here someone is being open, is abandoning the conventional pattern of thought? But sometimes don't gestures of pastoral concern irritate us? In particular, doesn't perfectly staged emotional involvement keep us at a distance? Aren't we often uncertain whether we are encountering the preacher in person or the preacher's style? Or is it impossible to separate the two? For human beings also set their own scene. But they are more than that!

Or do we detect authenticity where a preacher explicitly refers back to experiences and sufferings in speaking personally? But anyone with some knowledge of human nature who has listened to sermons knows that in them we do not meet the life of the other in undistorted openness but always only in a particular stylized form. The person of the sermon is not simply identical with the real biographical person; this person is the person that the preacher wants to present to the congregation: a selection, a one-sided picture. And that is a good thing: it would be painful if the sermon gave us a psychological picture of the preacher instead of a message.

We should recognize clearly that the person of the preacher as experienced in the sermon is a stylized person.[17] The authenticity of the preacher is a matter of balance between self-revelation and self-stylization. What has to be criticized is not the fact of this stylization, but its manner. We need to ask: can preachers bring their lives and their commitment into a sermon in such a way that both are given exemplary and representative significance? So that others recognize themselves in the preacher? So that wider structures of life and faith are recognizable in the person of the preacher? This kind of personal style is necessary. The subjective authenticity of the sermon does not consist in a direct account of the 'unwashed' subjectivity of the preacher, but in the deliberate shaping of the preacher's own thought, feeling and life in a direction which could also be valid for others. But that is not the preacher's whole life. So the rule of thumb here is not simply that preachers should say only what they really think and bear witness to what has found an echo in their lives. It must be supplemented with a further principle: preachers need not say all that they think. They need not incorporate all their concerns into the sermon. There are sometimes questions and problems which they are not yet able to frame 'objectively', in order to raise them above the atmosphere of their own limited subjectivity.

But what is to be included in sermons? Certainly not just the problems and experiences which preachers believe they have grasped perfectly. Here, too, the principle of measured discrepancy applies. There are problems and experiences with which we have never finished, but with which we can cope responsibly. That can be demonstrated in two directions. First, in dealing with role expectations (of the pastor), and secondly, in dealing with the un-Christian 'shadow' that we all have, i.e. with those spheres of life which contradict the usual expectations of Christian faith and Christian life. Authenticity is shown in dealing with two complementary sides, with the role of the preacher and the preacher's un-Christian shadow.

It is a great mistake to think that authenticity is shown only by breaking through role expectations, and that life in accordance with preconceived expectations is intrinsically inauthentic. A simple reflection contradicts this. We have deliberately chosen the role of preacher. No one has forced us to do so. Anyone who can stylize his or her own self only by emphasizing this role loses credibility: such a person should either look for another profession or come clean on why he or she identifies with this role despite all the problems. Here an individualistic society nowhere expects total identification with a role. This identification will always only be partial. A degree of distancing from a role is part of role expectation today; a good teacher may not just be a teacher; a good politician may not be just a politician; a good president not just a president; a good pastor not just a pastor. A measured deviation from role expectations is desirable.

On the other hand, there is the question of dealing with the preacher's shadow. In everyone there is a corner which not only has not been Christianized but in which there is a hidden mistrust of Christianity – a repudiation of some things which are valuable and important to others. Preachers can assume that this is the case with many people in the congregation. If they work intensively on this problem themselves and mature in it, they can become models of how others, too, can deal with their 'shadow'.[18] The preacher may show that he or she inwardly suffers friction with some spheres of tradition and the church. But preachers should deliberately decide on the spheres they choose. At any rate I found very credible a Catholic priest who complained at an ecumenical wedding, 'There were church laws there which were harsh and which are sore points for all of us.'

We encounter the problem of authenticity in different forms with the other criteria. For the anxiety of preachers consists in the fact that respect for the faith of the community drives them into a conflict with the duty to be honest which cannot be resolved and that the tensions with the general awareness of Christian truth and norms become too great: say between historical criticism and traditional dogmatics.

3. Respect for fellow men and women

Any successful communication presupposes respect for the identity of others. That means that we should examine our language and actions not only to see whether we are all of a piece but also how these actions relate to the norms and convictions of our fellow human beings. No one has the right to keep on speaking or acting without first reflecting on the reactions of others.

The preacher seeks consensus. Respect and esteem are easier where we know that we agree with our counterpart on fundamental questions. Therefore it is an important task for every preacher to detect the shared convictions and values that lie deeper than manifest divergences. The list of basic motifs of Christian faith compiled above should help here. It is not final. It can be supplemented. But it refers back to basics in such a way as to be capable of infiltrating the opposition between liberal and conservative trends in the church and theology. And in particular, it can help to maintain and manifest mutual respect even beyond differences.

However, the respect to be communicated in every sermon goes beyond this. It is aimed not at what consensus can be achieved on but at the whole person. It has the character of love.[19] Love knows that the beloved has strange sides, aspects which are difficult to take – but nevertheless holds fast to the beloved. How can the preacher show such respect?

Any sermon can express empathy. That is particularly true of the spheres of life which are bracketted out of everyday public language. It is true of the many unacknowledged anxieties and longings which accompany, permeate and torment everyday life, and which are not communicated to others. For example, there is the longing for love and tenderness (often in the form of fantasies which do not relate to the real partner). There is anxiety about sickness or death. Or anxiety about failure to achieve or the need to win through against opposition. Or there is simply the shame in which people imprison themselves because they are the only ones to have a particular problem. Or deep-seated resentment at the injustice of fate, and so on. Most people keep such anxieties and longings under control in their everyday lives. They have a direct effect on everyday life only where there is a high degree of neurosis. In this respect, too, the preacher may be an incomplete person. Unless preachers sense all these anxieties and longings in themselves, how are they to address them credibly? Unless they are themselves open to the unknown aspect of life, how can they help others to become open to it? This is matched by my observation that good preachers – especially preachers who seem 'emotional' – are often highly neurotic. Balanced people who are at ease with themselves often calmy avoid the diffuse emotional background of life.

Empathy is bound up with acceptance. But acceptance goes beyond this. It is not just a matter of understanding those small longings which are often so powerful, but of accepting life as it is actually lived. It evades the normative conditions of church and society. An important task of preaching is to create a climate of acceptance for the whole range of real behaviour. This then paradoxically also includes acceptance of the 'normal case'. For in modern permissive societies the person whose life takes a 'normal' course often finds this course difficult to explain. Why is he still married to his first wife? Has something gone wrong – or is he just sweeping some problems under the carpet? There is no doubt today that sometimes those who live unassuming lives, to whom society owes so much, need some 'stroking'.

Respect for the congregation also involves accepting its expectations of the preacher. For here we find ourselves in direct interaction. The congregation has come to hear a sermon. But this very expectation is bound up with wishes which in themselves ask too much – and contain a great potential for conflict and disappointment. These expectations are:

First, of professional competence: the preacher has studied the Bible and knows about the church and theology. This is a justified expectation, even if it is often not fulfilled because of many failings in the course of study.

Furthermore, the preacher should be a representative of the faith. At least in the view of the congregation, the preacher should have coped with all the dilemmas and problems which burden Christian faith: grappling with ideological devaluation, historical criticism and scientific scepticism.

But above all the preacher is still expected to have charisma. The preacher is expected to have an inexplicable aura – an aura in which the presence of the holy can be detected. For many people, the preacher is transcendence within their reach. And who could live up to such an expectation?

Respect for the expectations of the community calls for two things: meeting such expectations, but also correcting them. No preacher is theologically omniscient; no preacher has finished with questions of faith; no preacher has the charisma of the holy, except in very earthly and questionable vessels. Respect for others continually involves a reminder that preachers are real people.

Respect for fellow human beings is inconceivable without empathy and acceptance. But it does not end there. I also show my respect for others by criticizing them. Respect for a congregation includes the freedom to confront them with an idea which one knows some will reject and of which some will probably never be persuaded. Anyone who avoids confrontation with the congregation in principle is not respecting it. The more reliable the positive basic attitude is, the more confrontation the preacher can risk. There is certainly also an element of aggression here. Tact and humour can make the aggression more acceptable, but they cannot silence it. Respect for fellow human beings is therefore always a matter of balancing acceptance and confrontation, empathy and detached courtesy, which maintains a distance, intimacy and remoteness. Only disparaging aggression destroys relationships. It is destructive when someone involuntarily signals, 'I think nothing of you, find you intolerable.' Such justified criticism can then lead to a hardening of attitudes. And the preacher would also be responsible for this. That brings us to our last communicative value: responsibility.

4. Responsibility

Who would deny that preachers are also responsible for the consequences of their words? And that they therefore must always keep this in mind when preaching? Yet we have both pre-modern and modern theories at our disposal to relieve us of responsibility. Traditional theological dogmatics says that the Holy Spirit is ultimately responsible for the effect of preaching. Modern communication theories claim that in any case hearers use a great many filters to allow into themselves only what they need.[20] Preaching appears as a kind of metaphysical relief enterprise to unburden life of insoluble relics of problems so that it can continue as before.

This limit to our power as preachers is a scandal and a trial for many theologians. Do not the churches of the Reformation in particular live by the conviction that the Word of God is a power which can change life? But the Word of God becomes effective only through faith, i.e. through the free assent of the individual, without any compulsion – including psychological compulsion. At the time of the Reformation there was a threat of psychological compulsion in the form of anxiety about the punishments of hell. As word and faith became the decisive communication of salvation, the anxiety engendered by the late mediaeval church system was exploded. At that time preaching had liberating power. But today are we not experiencing above all its impotence?

In the face of the limits which are constantly experienced, and which every preacher gets to know, it may seem paradoxical to argue that preaching should limit itself. It should have an influence on life but at the same time communicate the message that in the last resort it is the hearers who decide what affects their lives and what does not.

One can illustrate the problem from sermons with an ethical orientation. They are indispensable. Anyone who dismisses them as 'legalistic' is missing the point of such sermons, as of life. Today sermons on the Ten Commandments are still given everywhere. In one of these series I had the task of preaching on the commandment 'You shall not commit adultery'.[21] I was aware that here the sermon was intervening in a sphere which people nowadays claim for themselves and defend as a free area. No one wants neighbours, state or church to speak in it. The sermon was advertised in the town as part of the whole series. I heard that some people were saying 'We're not going. We don't want to hear anything about that.' Nevertheless, the church was fuller than average. My sermon was a balance between acceptance and orientation. On the one hand – also according to my own convictions – I had to accept the various norms of life which have developed. On the other hand – also according to my convictions – I had to make it clear why for me marriage is an image of a covenant with being which extends far beyond the human dimension. I hope that everyone felt that I was respecting the decision for other forms of life, and that in them I detect a struggle for a humane form of life in which the norms and values that I too share are at work. I am convinced that in this way I argued more effectively for marriage than by a sermon which spoke about marriage without any alternative. One sign that I did was that some of those who had said that (for the reasons mentioned above) they would not be coming to church to hear my sermon, got hold of the text afterwards. They certainly didn't read it in order to see their decision justified in retrospect.

It is possible that the community in a university city reacts differently in this respect from elsewhere. It is often said that ordinary people need clear directions. So one has to speak with authority. I am sceptical. Both simple and educated people need clear guidance, and both allow their spheres of freedom to be limited only under protest. But these spheres of freedom look different in different social milieus. What are real options in a university city are remote possibilities in other areas. But within any area of life there are alternatives. Within any social and moral milieu decisions must be made, as they must be within a limited sphere of life.

Here the same problem arises everywhere: people struggle in the face of several possibilities to preserve their freedom even when inwardly they opt for a particular possibility. Those who decree a possibility (which they prefer) and say that there is no alternative come up against resistance. Psychology calls that 'reactance', everyday psychology calls it 'obstinacy'. But in both cases there is an awareness that something which a person has been able to decide freely will be more of a permanent element in his or her life than something imposed from outside.

We have been discussing the problem in terms of an ethical decision. However, it applies to all decisions. It is equally true of the basic decision about Christianity. Nothing is achieved here with psychological compulsion and social pressure. On the contrary, the experience of once having felt alienated from the church and faith while being closely connected with it makes people fight all their lives for great inward and outward detachment.

Preaching responsibly means reflecting on the influence and limits of the sermon. Within these limits the preacher has a great responsibility. Preachers do not perceive this responsibility if they force on others what is important and valuable to themselves. They perceive it when they strike a balance between a clear orientation and respect for the freedom of the other, including the freedom of the other to avoid what they are saying.

Luther once made a remark about this problem which is worth thinking about. He was talking about a missionary who wanted to convert a country but did not win a single person over to the Christian faith. The missionary complained about his fate. But Luther reprimanded him with the words, 'It is a sure sign of a bad will that he can't take being thwarted.'

C. The presupposition for successful communication: concern for the truth

Communication succeeds only if everyone takes the objective truth seriously. That is true of communication in all spheres. Communication in economics must submit to the criteria of economic rationality; communication in the legal sphere to the law; communication in the political sphere can succeed only in the framework and the spirit of the constitution. There is also a distinctive theological 'rationality' in the church. But in addition it is true of all spheres that there is a general human awareness of the truth which cannot be regionalized. It has a special place in the church, as it relates to God who is present in all spheres of reality. This desire for the truth makes dissent and conflict tolerable. The presupposition is that both sides allow themselves to be governed in the conflict by a concern for the truth. As long as this is the case, there is a basis for inter-personal respect – and a counterbalance against all violations which result in conflicts.

For preaching, we can concentrate on a particular problem which can become acute in many sermons. Historical and anthropological enlightenment about the Bible and religion can involve the average Christian consciousness in a deep hermeneutical conflict. Only a few members of a congregation will be aware that historical criticism regards many letters of the New Testament as 'inauthentic'. They are pseudepigrapha, i.e. they are attributed to a false author – and not always simply in good faith but sometimes with a deliberate suggestion of authenticity (one could even say, with an intent to deceive). Only a few members of a congregation will be aware that the myth of the lawgiving on Sinai is a remarkable fiction, remarkable because it gave the law as the foundation of an independent form of Jewish life an origin and a legitimation independent of any state legislation, which made life under the Torah possible even under the conditions of alien rule. Similarly, not everyone knows the full impact of historical criticism on the traditions about Jesus – regardless of the fact that this criticism often left the limits of historical plausibility and itself created a new aura of scientific fictions around Jesus. The imperative for truth which is alive in the church rules out the expedient of claiming two truths: a limited truth for the community and an enlightened truth for theologians. Rather, the task is to gain an understanding of the specific truth of fictional language in the Bible (and in all religious traditions) – in other words, an understanding of biblical poetry, a sense of the 'poetry of the sacred', which covers everything in the Bible with a delicate veil – including the undoubted historical situations and events to which the Bible bears witness.

Here the task in the religious tradition differs somewhat from that in genuine poetry – even where in our eyes the former is poetry. Genuine poetry does not conceal its fictional character. Everyone approaches it in the expectation of entering into a world of meanings which is a human invention, i.e. has been created by fantasy. Mature treatment of great poetry recognizes the reality in these fictional texts and puts delight in knowledge communicated poetically above pleasure in the beautiful and the pleasing. Great poetry is painful and tragic and gives form to the absurd. It is not beautiful and pleasing.

In religious texts the starting point is different. They confront us with the tradition's claim to be true and real. They do not seek to take us into a fictional world, but into a real history of God and human beings. Here the process of maturing lies in the capacity of hearer and reader to recognize increasingly clearly the fictional aura which is almost omnipresent in the narratives and traditions and to see it, not as lies, deception and nonsense but as an extension of reality, a growth in human freedom.

But how can one communicate that to the average congregation without causing deep discomfort? It is better not to start any clarification of insight into the truth of the fictional by referring to biblical texts, but to use texts which one has composed oneself. Here everyone can experience the process of 'composition' before their eyes. Then one can go on to biblical texts. I cannot go on to discuss all the forms of fictionality in the Bible, so here I shall content myself with mythical, legendary and pseudepigraphical texts.

To demonstrate the function of some myths, I would like to relate a fictional anecdote about uncle Hubertus and his nephew Hubert. Uncle Hubertus had a remarkably long nose, for which he was mocked from his childhood on. His small nephew Hubert asked him in childlike innocence, 'Why do you have such a big nose? Why do other people have different noses – like mine?' His uncle replied, 'It was like this. When noses were being distributed at our creation the two of us were last. When I saw your nose, of course I reached for it. But the Creator said quite firmly, "Don't touch that nose. That's a rotten nose. I've another here which suits you. Take it. It's the best nose in the world."'

What can we learn from this short creation myth? That myths help us to cope with contingency, in this case a remarkably large nose which became almost a stigma for uncle Hubertus. The story itself is fiction. But the big nose and its social repudiation is reality, the reality that our own bodies are not at our disposal. However, the fictional myth turns this reality with its needs and limitations into freedom: the person concerned accepts his life as though he had wanted it to be like that and not otherwise. The aura of fictionality creates freedom.

We can also transfer this insight to the biblical creation story. It has mythical features, even if it is clearly different from the myths widespread in the ancient Near East. For us, it is decisive that here, too, there is a value judgment on the end of creation, 'And behold, it was very good.' The aim of the narrative is for the hearer to endorse this judgment. The existence of the world and its structure are given contingently. But assent to it is a free decision.

As a second example I have chosen a legendary text – a text which is attached to an undoubtedly historical figure, but which is itself unhistorical. When such a story is set in a predominantly secular milieu we speak of a saga. When it is set in a church milieu, the term 'legend' is better. But we are not concerned with the difference. The starting point is a family legend from modern times. There is a tradition in a German family that the great-grandfather went to Holland during the 1870/71 war so as not to have to take part in the war against France. The family is proud of its ancestor, since it is opposed to war. One of the great-grandsons studies history. He applies his historical-critical tools to the family tradition. In so doing, he discovers that at the time of the Franco-Prussian war the great-grandfather was only fifteen. His supposed stay in Holland cannot have been motivated by a desire to avoid military service. It is not certain whether he was in Holland at that time. Moreover the great-grandson discovers that the family legend about the pacifist great-grandfather is told only after 1919. Perhaps it is a fictitious history with which the family reacted to the terrors of the First World War. Should the family then completely 'demythologize' the grandfather? Or should it unswervingly keep to the real message of the family legend, the repudiation of war? This kerygma is in fact independent of the historicity of the tradition. Or may it start from the fact that this repudiation of the war has support in the historical great-grandfather? For regardless of whether or not he was in Holland in 1870/71, there is evidence from a later time which allows the inference of a pacifist attitude. Here, too, sense can be made of the aura of fictionality surrounding the great-grandfather: a family with a pacifist attitude is looking for allies among its forebears. Such allies are important for anchoring its own values firmly in the identity of the family – and creating a greater independence from their setting for them: freedom from the militaristic climate in large parts of German society beween 1914 and 1945. Fictional and historical elements are here fused into an indissoluble unity.

The stories of the infancy of Jesus in the Gospels of Matthew and Luke are to be assessed in a similar way to these family legends. Their theme is the relationship of the new 'king' born in Bethlehem

to the real ruler who was ruling at the time: to Herod (Matthew) and
to Augustus (Luke). They show two possible reactions to these
rulers: flight from persecution (Matthew) and obedience to the command to register in a census (Luke). Both infancy narratives transfer
the birth of Jesus, contrary to historical reality, to Bethlehem. For the
future ruler of Israel was to come from Bethlehem (Micah
5.1ff. = Matt.2.6). It is necessary for him to be born there to make it
possible to depict the contrast between the true ruler of Israel and the
political powers. At all events, the newborn child is the superior ruler.
At all events, the Christian community may take its bearings from
him – and be aware that it is free in the face of political rulers,
whether it finds these hostile (Matthew) or neutral (Luke). Here, too,
there is a historical nucleus: the historical Jesus proclaimed the kingdom of God which was superior to all political rule. The aura of
fictionality surrounding his birth is intended to strengthen the freedom of his successors from political power.

Finally, an example of pseudepigraphical texts. Preaching has many
opportunities to create pseudepigraphical texts. That happens if one
playfully formulates a homiletical commentary in the form of a fictitious
letter of Paul or invents replies from early Christians to Paul's letters.
Why is it homiletically so fruitful to slip into the role of a fictitious other?
The answer is obvious. In this indirect way one can confront the
congregation with statements which are very much bolder than they
could be if they were direct statements. The community has the
freedom to repudiate the statement of the fictitious author. It can tell
itself that the preacher is just playing games. But what is said can also be
enlightening. The congregation can then make it its own. It agrees with
the content, although it sees through the fictitious game with the
invented author, in other words despite a plausible opportunity for
people to distance themselves from what is being said. Now in the case
of the biblical pseudepigraphical works one can argue that these do not
present their fictitious character openly. They conceal it. In some
writings like the Pastoral Epistles, authenticity is suggested in an almost
refined way (so that biblical critics keep arguing for their authenticity,
down to the present day). Nevertheless, the process of reception in
earliest Christianity was comparable to the reception of a sermon which
plays with pseudepigraphical texts. The content was the deciding factor.
If this content was accepted positively, people in antiquity were
amazingly generous over questions of authenticity. However, if the
content was rejected, the authenticity of the relevant writing tended to be

put in question.[22] Thus for a long time there was a dispute over whether the Letter to the Hebrews was really written by Paul. That did not get in the way of its acceptance into the canon. It content was accepted. Conversely, the Gospel of John was widely accepted. Only when the Montanists appealed to it was its apostolic origin put in question: suddenly it was regarded as a creation of the heretic Cerinthus.

It needs a certain maturity of judgment to recognize the aura of fictionality that surrounds history – in very different ways – throughout the Bible. Once one has recognized it, one has a duty to make it evident to ordinary people. That is not very easy. One obstacle at least may be mentioned. People who are not directly involved in the process of academic or scientific study often tend towards a naive antithesis between 'reliable science' and 'fictional witnesses'. They fail to recognize that scholarship does not get through to pure historical truth. Rather, with its many hypotheses and perspectivistic images, basically it tends to produce a new modern 'aura of fictionality' around past history. The quest of the historical Jesus is a good example of that.[23] And yet that does not make scholarship valueless. Rather, there is no disputing the fact that one and the same figure encounters us through the modern aura of fictionality.

This can be demonstrated by the following test. Take all the academic books about Jesus. They all contain pictures of him which are one-sided in their perspective. Then delete all the proper names from the books so that they become anonymous. An unprejudiced reader does not know whom they are about, where and when they take place. Nevertheless, I am certain that among all the books a group of books will seem to belong together, which refer to the figure of Jesus. For all are using the same sources, utilizing the same tradition, reacting to the same 'contradictions' in them.

We can arrive at the following provisional summary. We owe it to our modern awareness of truth to show up the aura of fictionality in the biblical text. We also owe it to this awareness of truth to show clearly the degree to which fictionality serves the truth.

In all this we have subjected preaching first to a general awareness of truth. Over and above that, in the sphere of the church, are there not specific norms of truth – a truth which emerges from its special subject? I do not intend to make a plea for a twofold truth, one inside and one outside the church, but to recognize the fact that in a modern society all spheres of life have developed specific norms. In science the strict criteria of true and false apply; in business the criteria of profit and loss;

in art the criteria of the aesthetic and the unaesthetic. Evey sphere of life organizes itself by its own laws.

Religion is a sign language which makes possible an awareness among human groups of aiming at an enhancement of life by corresponding with an ultimate reality. In the course of history it has increasingly clearly developed a tendency to organize itself by its own point of reference. Originally it was inextricably bound into a whole culture. Religions were sign languages in which tribes and peoples assured themselves of their identity. But with the rise of high religions they became independent. They detached themselves from the particular groups which had created them. Rather, they gained new groups for themselves, indeed they created new groups. In this way the earliest Christian sign system detached itself from Judaism. It integrated people of quite different cultural and national origins. It produced a new form of human community: the church which was not identical with society. But above all, this new sign system increasingly clearly claimed to be organized from its own centre. Everything valid in it is to be understood as an expression of its relationship with God: as the consequence of a revelation.

In modern society the Christian sign system again had to detach itself from being embedded in the life of society as a whole in a way which was taken for granted. Since then theology and church have been struggling for their autonomy. What claims space in the church can no longer just claim legitimation by tradition and origin. Within Protestantism it can be justified only by the word of God, i.e. by a sign language of faith which creates contact with an ultimate reality. Therefore every sermon makes a specific theological claim to truth: it falls short of its goal if it offers pedagogical, psychotherapeutical or social ethical reflections, however good they may be. These are certainly part of preaching. But preaching draws its own dynamic from its subject: it seeks to lead to a fusion between dialogue with God and dialogue among human beings – also in the dialogue about problems of education, psychotherapy and social ethics. Only in this way does preaching become the sign language of faith. But the truth of such a sign language lies in its basic motifs, in learned patterns of experience and behaviour which are effective *a priori* in our life, and in the light of which reality becomes transparent to an ultimate reality. Truth is a matter of corresponding to this reality. Truth is a matter of matching life to God. It is served by myths and legends, the fictional and the historical, parables and images, reflections on education and social ethics, therapy and the universe. And these homiletical reflections, too, seek to serve truth.

VI

Examples of Preaching

1. Simon the Tanner and Simon Peter
A sermon on Acts 10.1–35
(Petra von Gemünden)

Cornelius the centurion

At Caesarea there was a man named Cornelius, a centurion of what was known as the Italian cohort, a devout man who feared God with all his household, gave alms liberallly to the people, and prayed constantly to God. About the ninth hour of the day he saw clearly in a vision an angel of God coming in and saying to him, 'Cornelius.' And he stared at him in terror, and said, 'What is it, Lord?' And he said to him, 'Your prayers and your alms have ascended as a memorial before God. And now send men to Joppa, and bring one Simon who is called Peter; he is lodging with Simon, the tanner, whose house is by the seaside.' When the angel who spoke to him had departed, he called two of his servants and a devout soldier from among those that waited on him, and having related everything to them, he sent them to Joppa.

The next day, as they were on their journey and coming near the city, Peter went up on the housetop to pray, about the sixth hour. And he became hungry and desired something to eat; but while they were preparing it, he fell into a trance and saw the heaven opened, and something descending, like a great sheet, let down by four corners upon the earth. In it were all kinds of animals and reptiles and birds of the air. And there came a voice to him, 'Rise, Peter; kill and eat.' But Peter said, 'No, Lord; for I have never eaten anything that is common or unclean.' And the voice came to him again a second time, 'What God has cleansed, you must not call common.' This happened three times, and the thing was taken up at once to heaven.

Now while Peter was inwardly perplexed as to what the vision which he had seen might mean, behold, the men that were sent by Cornelius, having made enquiry for Simon's house, stood before the gate and called out to ask whether Simon who was called Peter was lodging there. And while Peter was pondering the vision, the Spirit said to him, 'Behold, three men are looking for you. Rise and go down, and accompany them without hesitation; for I have sent them.' And Peter went down to the men and said, 'I am the one you are looking for; what is the reason for your coming?' And they said, 'Cornelius, a centurion, an upright and god-fearing man, who is well spoken of by the whole Jewish nation, was directed by a holy angel to send for you to come to his house, and to hear what you have to say.' So he called them in to be his guests.

The next day he arose and went off with them, and some of the brethren from Joppa accompanied him. And on the following day they entered Caesarea. Cornelius was expecting them and had called together his kinsmen and close friends. When Peter entered, Cornelius met him and fell down at his feet and worshipped him. But Peter lifted him up, saying, 'Stand up; I too am a man.' And as he talked with him, he went in and found many persons gathered; and he said to them, 'You yourselves know how unlawful it is for a Jew to associate with or to visit any one of another nation; but God has shown me that I should not call any man common or unclean. So when I was sent for, I came without objection. I ask then why you sent for me.'

And Cornelius said, 'Four days ago, about this hour, I was keeping the ninth hour of prayer in my house; and behold a man stood before me in bright apparel, saying, "Cornelius, your prayer has been heard and your alms have been remembered before God. Send therefore to Joppa and ask for Simon who is called Peter; he is lodging in the house of Simon, a tanner, by the seaside." So I sent to you at once and you have been kind enough to come. Now therefore we are all here present in the sight of God, to hear all that you have been commanded by the Lord.'

And Peter opened his mouth and said: 'Truly I perceive that God shows no partiality, but in every nation anyone who fears him and does what is right is acceptable to him.'

I want to let someone else speak today. Someone who can tell the story of Cornelius the centurion in quite a different way. He's not exactly well known, since he appears in only three verses in the New Testament: Simon the Tanner. At first he had doubts about speaking to us today, because he's just a simple man from Palestine, but I thought it would be a good thing for him to do so. For earliest Christianity was a movement of simple, insignificant people, and it is in keeping with Christian faith to take the perspective of the insignificant, the outsiders, and those who come off worst. So I will step down and allow Simon the Tanner to speak:

Dear people, you should know that I'm just a small tradesman; indeed, less than that – I'm a tanner. Everyone avoids tanners. 'They stink,' people say and give them a wide berth. 'They're unclean,' say the

Jews, and treat us like tax-collectors. But we too are Jews. At least the tax-collectors earn more than we do – and they can do a lot with their money. Whereas we have to work with animal corpses and urine, day in, day out, for a starvation wage. You need to know that only urine makes leather soft. 'Dead bodies make you unclean.' 'Animal corpses and piss stink terribly,' people say, and they're right. But how else can I make leather? My job left me quite isolated in the city. No one wanted to have anything to do with me. I hardly ever met my kinsfolk. That first changed when a Christian community began in our city. 'Come to me, all of you,' this Jesus, their Lord, is said to have said. He is said to have been concerned with outsiders and the sick. And so they also made a place for me when I came. Although I never really got rid of the terrible smell, they were friendly to me. None of them turned up their noses. Not even the rich ladies and the respectable merchants who were also among them. I had never experienced anything like it before. It was as though there were no longer any boundaries between people from the upper classes and those from the lower classes; as though all professions were equally valuable and important. Can you imagine what it meant to me? I, the tanner whom everyone despised, at last belonged. I was someone again, although I couldn't give much to the collection. So I remained with the community and began to pray to the one who can produce such remarkable changes. I prayed to the one who stopped at no frontiers, not even the frontier of death.

And one day – just imagine, one day the great apostle Peter came from Jerusalem to our city of Joppa by the Mediterranean. You probably know that Peter was the one who went around with our Lord Jesus Christ. And later I even heard that it was said in Matthew's community, 'On this rock I will build my church.' And in John's community they told how Jesus said to this Peter, 'Feed my sheep.' Be that as it may, this Peter came to us. And do you know with whom he stayed? With me. He stayed with the stinking tanner. The famous missionary was a guest of mine, a guest of the one whom everyone had once avoided. When he saw my anxious face, he just laughed and said, 'Simon, my brother, you know I was once a fisherman, and now I'm a fisher of men and women, so your smell won't put me off.' And he just came. That's how I got to hear the story of the Roman centurion Cornelius, who converted our highly-respected missionary Peter. Yes, you can put it like that – this Cornelius, who wasn't even a Jew or a Christian, converted our apostle Peter. At that time there was a change which one might call revolutionary – I think even more revolutionary than the change that you people here, living on the border with East Germany, have been experiencing now that it has been opened up. Indeed, I would venture to say that had it not been for this foreigner Cornelius, you wouldn't be in church today, simply because in that case the good news of Jesus Christ wouldn't have got beyond a small circle of Jewish Christians. And if I'm right, none of you are Jews.

But back to the story about Cornelius. I got quite excited. For one day shortly before lunch there was a knock at my door. I opened it and had the fright of my life: there were three men standing outside, a Roman soldier and two slaves. 'Is Simon called Peter staying here?' they asked. I immediately thought of the persecution of some Christians in Jerusalem which had recently driven the Christians westwards, also towards Joppa. Just as I was going to say, 'I'm sorry, there's no Simon Peter here,' unfortunately Peter came down the stairs. I thought, 'Now it's all up,' and at the same time heard the voice of Peter behind me. 'I'm the one you're looking for. Why are you here?' What they then said seemed to me to be very obscure. They related how a Roman officer in the garrison city of Caesarea called Cornelius had sent them and invited the great missionary and apostle to go to his house. Was this a trick? A peaceful arrest? Did a member of the Roman occupying forces – the very occupying forces who had executed Jesus – want to invite a Jew like Peter into his house? And if he really lived a pious and godfearing life, prayed regularly and gave alms and therefore was respected by the Jews in his city as they said, didn't he know that a pious Jew would never enter the house of a Gentile, because that would make him unclean? And as an officer, he couldn't be circumcised and become a Jew, or a Christian either, because – as every child knows – he had to recognize and worship the emperor as his lord. Moreover being an officer is a military profession, a profession in which one even has to kill. And such professions are forbidden to us Christians. Therefore no Christian can be an executioner or a soldier. Later, things were to change. In the third century, under the emperor Constantine. Then they painted the cross on their standards and believed, 'In this sign you will conquer.' Even in your century there are said still to have been people who had 'God with us' on their military belt buckles. But right at the beginning it was very different. Very rigorous. It was clear that a Christian could have nothing to do with the military. And now we were to go into the house of a pagan soldier. That was too much to ask of Christians! Or more probably, a trap.

So I was all the more amazed when Peter asked the three in in a friendly way and gave them something to eat. And that evening he managed to persuade some of the brothers from the church to go with him next day. He told us how shortly before noon God had spoken to him on the roof in a dream. God had shown him clean and unclean animals all together and said, 'Eat!' And when he had objected, 'I have never yet eaten anything unholy and unclean,' God's voice had answered him. 'Don't call unclean what God has declared clean!' And when the men had knocked at the door, the voice had said to him, 'Get up, go down, and don't hesitate to go with them, for I have sent them.' And I don't know why – was it Peter's power of persuasion, or the obligations of a host? – I went too.

There we were in Caesarea, and everything happened very quickly. Cornelius and his household were very courteous. As he spoke, we all suddenly felt, 'God is also here with this Gentile. He is also here with this Roman officer. With this foreigner, who has grown up in a quite different culture and speaks and lives so differently from us.' And all at once it dawned on Peter what God wanted to make clear to him through Cornelius, through this centurion who was neither Jew nor Christian. God is very much greater than we can see and understand. His love knows no frontiers. God does not recognize social, professional or ideological frontiers. Not even the frontiers of belonging to a people. For God is Lord of all men and women; his gospel is for all. God 'has no respect of persons'. That made me, the despised tanner, think of myself and my life. And then I understood: God's spirit wants to overcome the frontiers which divide us human beings so painfully. Against the background of the mission to the Gentiles which began at that time, I can say that we Jewish Christians wanted to preserve the gospel by anxiously protecting it from being swamped and being made unclean. But the gospel could not develop its power in that way, because it consists in overcoming limits of character, class, profession, nation and thus making life possible. It took a foreign Gentile to show us that.

I don't know you very well, dear people, but perhaps you might like to ask yourselves whether sometimes you don't keep God shut up in your church walls, whether sometimes you're not tempted to associate with Christians of a particular political attitude or with whom you get on well. I want to bring you the good news that God is greater, infinitely greater. Perhaps you might discover that one day, as we did: in conversation with an atheist or a Buddhist, with someone seeking asylum, a drop-out or a successful businessman, an old person or a child. I tell you, the Spirit blow where it wills. And the Spirit may open up a new understanding of

God where no one expects it. For the love of God does not recognize any frontiers. It seeks to take hold of all men and women. So let me end with the wish that we expressed at the end of all our worship in Joppa. May the peace of God which passes all our understanding, keep our hearts and minds in Christ Jesus. That is my wish, too.

A sermon preached in Coburg on 21 January 1990. Life there had been fundamentally changed by the opening of the frontier with East Germany in November 1989. A city in a 'dead corner' next to the frontier had turned into a city heavily visited by East Germans, with far-reaching consequences for business life, the social system, the labour market and educational institutions.

2. The judge of the world right down there
A sermon on Matt.25.31–46
(*Petra von Gemünden*)

When the Son of man comes in his glory, and all the angels with him, then he will sit on his glorious throne. Before him will be gathered all the nations, and he will separate them from one another as a shepherd separates the sheep from the goats, and he will place the sheep at his right hand, but the goats at the left. Then the King will say to those at his right hand, 'Come, O blessed of my Father, inherit the kingdom prepared for you from the foundation of the world; for I was hungry and you gave me food; I was thirsty, and you gave me drink, I was a stranger and you welcomed me, I was naked and you clothed me, I was sick and you visited me, I was in prison and you came to me.' Then the righteous will answer him, 'Lord, when did we see you hungry and feed you, or thirsty and give you drink? And when did we see you a stranger and welcome you, or naked and clothe you? And when did we see you sick or in prison and visit you?' And the King will answer them, 'Truly, I say to you, as you did it to one of the least of these my brethren, you did it to me.'

Then he will say to those at his left hand, 'Depart from me, you cursed, into the eternal fire prepared for the devil and his angels; for I was hungry and you gave me no food; I was thirsty, and you gave me no drink, I was a stranger and you did not welcome me, naked and you did not clothe me, sick and in prison and you did not visit me.' Then they will also answer, 'Lord, when did we see you hungry or thirsty or a stranger or naked or in prison, and did not minister to you?' Then he will answer them, 'Truly, I say to you, as you did it not to one of the least of these, you did it not to me.' And they will go away into eternal punishment, but the righteous into eternal life.

When I read out the parable of the great judgment, a cold shiver ran through me: I met the gaze of a strict God of judgment, in whose eyes thousandfold distress, thousandfold dismay is expressed. The world was reflected in his sharp eyes, and I recognized that the judgment of the world, the eternal pain which Matthew speaks of in his parable about the judgment of the world, has long been there. The prophetic sounding words of the judge of the world, 'Away from me, you accursed, into the eternal fire,' have long since become reality in the fire of the cannons at Stalingrad, in the atomic bombing of Hiroshima and Nagasaki, in the blazing hatred which flares up in Northern Ireland, in the Middle East and in many other places on earth.

On a day of national mourning, the apocalyptic prophecy of the judge of the world, 'and they will go into eternal torment', has a quite special ring for me. I see the young soldiers marching enthusiastically behind the standards in the First World War, confident of victory, 'God with Us' shining on their belt buckles. So they marched into the hellish fire of exploding mines and burning grenades. They zealously dug trenches, trenches which were to protect them, trenches in which they could hide, trenches from which they could venture to attack, trenches which became graves for thousand upon thousand. I still remember how helpless bewilderment seized me when I went with French friends over the terrible earth of Verdun, covered in a cold cloud of fear. I noted with horror how close the trenches were together and yet how far people must have been from one another. What did one know of the joys and anxieties, the hopes and disappointments of the other? Often they didn't see one another at all, or only right in the distance – as scheming, threatening strangers, the enemy who brought death and destruction. Death and destruction everywhere. Meaningless. Empty. And not just here. A few years later they were dying in the icy wilderness of Siberia and in the hellishly hot African desert, in their thousands upon thousands, senselessly and uselessly. And every death tore an aching hole in families and friendships. I see all this in the eyes of the judge of the world: trenches crossing the earth, separating people into black and white, north and south, rich and poor, friend and foe, good and evil. I see trenches between us and the Third World, between us and immigrant workers: trenches that we dig deeper and deeper to cement our prosperity and our security. I see trenches fortified with prejudices and incomprehension, trenches between the successful and unsuccesful, between those in work and the unemployed.

I see trenches which can easily become graves: graves of the human, graves of humankind. I see how the world is moving towards an inferno of hellishly burning flames and the question escapes me, 'Where is God? Where is the God who intervenes with a mighty hand?' My cry echoes without being answered. Where is God? That was the desperate cry in Verdun, before Stalingrad and in Dachau. Where is God? I don't see him. I see the terror, the distress, the pain, but the God who helps – I cannot see him, recognize him, feel him: he is too remote up there away from me. I feel abandoned and alone. Separated by a deep gulf from up there. 'Does God exist at all,' I ask myself, 'the powerful God, almighty up there above the clouds?'

I do not see him. I do not hear him.

I sense only infinite burdensome silence.

I want to listen once again to the story of the great judgment of the world. There I hear the voice of the strict God of judgment up there, who shows up the trenches dug between people. But I also hear another voice, the voice of the one who has overcome the distance between God and human beings, who has become man in order to become a brother to humankind. He has crossed the trenches of hatred and indifference, of prejudice and anxiety, which gape between human beings: he has become open to the publicans and sinners, the outcast and the despised. He has become a brother to them – these strangers – in order to discover the brother in them.

In this way and not in any other, God has abolished the trenches which lie between human beings.

God has not destroyed them by intervening from a safe distance with the weapons of his omnipotence and power. No, he has destroyed the trenches in the world by exposing himself to them, going through them; quite simply, by looking for the person on the other side. So he went where precisely where human dignity dies in the trench warfare of world-views and power interests, where life and love have been buried under indifference and blindness. So consistently did he take the side of the victims of these trenches that those who thought that they could exist only under the protection of these deep trenches could not bear it, and nailed him to the cross. He went to the cross, where he cried out, 'My God, my God, why have you forsaken me?' There, on the cross, God did not remain dumb; there he cried out his answer, his answer to all

laments, all distress, all the trenches of this world. God did not answer
from above with a powerful voice; no, he answered from deepest need by
taking up the cry of tormented humankind; there he took the side of
suffering human beings to the end. There, in his suffering on the cross,
the God of humankind became a brother through and through. And so a
gliimmer of hope shines through there, in the suffering of the God who
has overcome the trenches of death: the sense of the brother in every
human being. The sense of the brotherly God who wants to meet men
and women beyond all the trenches:
- The sense of the brother in the tattered figure who comes up to me
  smelling of alcohol.
- The sense of the brother in the immigrant worker who is alien to me
  and makes me anxious.
- The sense of the brother, or better the sister, in the woman next door,
  who has become so strange and inaccessible, imprisoned as she is in
  her pain and her solitude.

I think that where the sense of the brother in the other person dawns,
the gulfs between brother and brother and sister and sister are
overcome. Very simply, without great efforts and achievements.

Here's an example. Years ago I had to look after a woman in hospital.
She lay there motionless, her face expressionless, with the mask of death
on it. She was far away from me. Although I visited her every day, she
was separated from me by an immeasurable distance. However, once
when I was putting some eau de Cologne on her, as I had often already
done, she woke up for a fraction of a second. The expressionless mask of
her face dropped for a tiny moment and all at once I sensed something of
her, her life, her nature: the barriers between us had fallen. From then
on I looked after the woman in a different way: I treated her not just as a
patient, but as a woman who had become my sister.

I believe that where this intimation dawns, this sense of the brother or
sister in a person, the world imperceptibly changes. It does so without
extraordinary efforts and achievements. The God who has become our
brother does not want those of us.

Our story tells neither of heroic actions nor of men and women who
have performed particular feats of faith. I read of people who have given
the hungry something to eat, the thirsty something to drink, and have
visited the sick. There is no mention of those who have won medals or
honours or of Christians who have been particularly zealous in going to
church and who have no trouble in saying the creed. No, the people in
our story acted in a completely human way. They met the most basic of

needs: food, drink, visiting. Without a great many words. No more and no less. I see these people and think to myself: being a true Christian consists in being a true human being. Beyond the limts of nationality and ideologies, family and confessions. No more and no less. And I think of an episode from my father's life, which he kept relating. Once, in the middle of the war, in the depths of Russia, a simple peasant woman gave him her last eggs. 'Moi sin', 'My son', she said to the German soldier, and told him of her son who had been killed in the war – hit by German bullets. A few eggs, a few words. That is not much, yet it is a great deal, for here a simple peasant woman met in an alien enemy soldier the hungry person, the brother, indeed the son, and for a moment a young soldier unexpectedly found a mother. A few eggs, a few words – that is not much, and yet it is a great deal. Imperceptibly it bridges deep gaps.

In the midst of the dark night of war, between the trenches and the frontiers, a light shines. God encounters men and women.

So today, on this day of mourning, the parable of the great judgment of the world contains a hopeful message. If we see all those trenches mirrored in the eyes of the judge of the world and are terrified; if we sense and discover beyond all the frontiers our brothers and sisters, then the frontiers fall. Then the future opens up. Then the kingdom of God takes place. Here and now. Gently and imperceptibly and yet uncannily full of hope. For there – in the face of the brother and the sister – Jesus seeks to encounter us and free us from the trenches which separate us. From trenches which threaten to be the grave of humankind, the grave of his sighing creation.

The strict God of judgment has become our brother. For through the judgment and out of the judgment he wills to save us for a future as his sisters and brothers. That is our hope. Amen.

A sermon preached in Munich on 17 November 1911. The risk of this sermon was that some hearers would be so trapped in the aporias of the first half of the sermon that during the sermon itself they could not get to the positive way of coping with them in the second half. The comment of a theologian on this sermon was significant, 'You can't have God dying in the pulpit!' But there would also have been problems in bracketting off the aporias: the sermon has the task of evoking and working on limit situations in life in the proteeted sphere of worship and in the context of Christian life. That is particularly true of sermons on solemn occasions.

3. The house of mourning and the house of life
A sermon on Mark 13.31–37
(*Petra von Gemünden*)

'Heaven and earth will pass away, but my words will not pass away. But of that day or that hour no one knows, not even the angels in heaven nor the Son, but only the Father. Take heed, watch; for you do not know when the time will come. It is like a man going on a journey, when he leaves home and puts his servants in charge, each with his work, and commands the doorkeeper to be on the watch. Watch therefore – for you do not know when the master of the house will come, in the evening, or at midnight, or at cockcrow, or in the morning – lest he come suddenly and find you asleep. And what I say to you I say to all: Watch.'

'Heaven and earth will pass away but my words will not pass away' – that sounds reassuring and comforting to me. For me, the promise 'My words will not pass away' is like a rock to rest on in stormy surf, a rock in raging chaos. Support and hope – that is what we need in our lives, particularly when we lose the ground under our feet, particularly when mourning, anxiety and emptiness threaten to swallow us up. 'My words will not pass away' – this promise from God is to comfort and encourage us. This promise of Jesus is to give us support when we remember the dead and our transitory existence. It seeks to give us courage to receive new every day and use with care the gift of with which the Father entrusts us, as an unrepeatable gift of God. So it is no coincidence that in the text God's promise 'My words will not pass away' is followed by the admonition, 'Watch', which I would like to translate, 'Live attentively.'

Now I think that the way from the dark chaos of the feelings, from the dull emptiness of mourning, to attentive life can be a long one, one on which we continually set out under the promising star of the faithfulness of God and at whose end stands God's last promise: 'Heaven and earth will pass away, but my words will not pass away.'

I imagine that this way was also long and difficult for the disciples. They had given up everything for Jesus. They had left their jobs and families and lived only for him. They had shared everything with him – their bread, their fish, their ideas. And now suddenly he was no longer there. That was incomprehensible for them. A rapid, cruel, bewildering death had snatched him away. They felt infinitely forsaken and alone,

betrayed and exposed, terribly hurt. How could he just have left them
when he was so important for them? How could God have allowed it?
The God whom he had called his Father? There was anger and rage and
aggression. Sometimes these were directed against the dead man who
had left them alone so miserably, sometimes against the God who had
let him perish so wretchedly, and then again against themselves, for not
always having lived up to him. Where they had failed him now came out.
And he could no longer comfort them with his warm voice. They sought
him and his nearness. Their loves and affection for him became even
more intense. He became even more ideal. The bond with him became
even stronger. Love and hatred, bitter tears and an emptiness in which
crying was impossible: sometimes these came one after the other,
sometimes together. Yet at a stroke everything in their lives had fallen
apart, not only inside them, but in the outside world also. Their previous
way of life had been abruptly destroyed. Had it been in vain?
Meaningless? Was it devalued in retrospect by the way in which it
ended? Many things kept going through their heads. Everything had
suddenly changed. How were things to go on? Were they to pack it all in?
Yield to resignation? Go away? Give in to mourning? Follow him to
death? Sometimes such ideas ran through their minds. Sometimes they
just wanted to give up. And then they forced themselves to pull
themselves together. To turn to life and its loud demands. Sometimes it
was wearisome. But sometimes it was also healthy, because it distracted
them. Nevertheless, for a long time, a very long time, their hearts and
minds were not really in their work, not really in the present with their
fellow men and women. They were too imprisoned in the past, or floated
off into the realm of imagination, into a land where what the world had
failed them in was possible.

The disciples found an image for their situation, an image which
today's text from the Bible gives us. They felt like servants in a great,
abandoned house without a master. A house which at a stroke had
become comfortless and empty. A house resounding with memories and
in which solitude, mourning and meaninglessness dwelt, choking all
life. But that is not all. Those are only the first strokes of the pencil. For
the disciples went on painting, painting with bright, shining colours,
colours which bear witness to a profound experience, a new discovery.
Certainly the house is abandoned – there is no quibbling over that. It has
been abandoned by its master – but he is not dead. No, the disciples
have become certain that he is alive. He has gone on a long journey, they
tell us in their picture. And not only that, he has appointed us his

representatives. We are now to hand on the love, the warmth and the understanding which we received so richly from him. His friendliness and his care are to fill the house. And the disciples are there for one another in the spirit of Jesus. His words and actions give them support and orientation. They accept one another and their fellow men and women. They serve one another, each with his or her gift. One is good at stoking ovens, another is good at listening, a third, lying there sick, quite specially becomes the bearer of Christian hope – simply by the way in which he bears his suffering. All at once it is no longer emptiness and comfortlessness that resound from the walls; laughter and hope break out in joyful song from many voices. The Lord is no longer there, but his spirit fills the house. The Lord is no longer there – but his warm voice echoes in the voice of his followers. The Lord is no longer there – but his love can be traced in the love of the disciples.

And the picture tells us something else. It tells us of a fascinating change of direction. The disciples no longer look back. No, the direction of their gaze has changed: they look forward in joyful expectation, towards the one who will return, will return to his house. And then, as John the apocalyptist later tells us, God will wipe away all tears, death will be no more, and there will be no more suffering nor crying nor pain, for the old has passed away. Then only one thing remains: God's constancy and faithfulness, God's love and providence for us, in short, all that he has promised us in word and deed through his son. That already applies now, and will prove truth and reality at the end of every life and at the end of the world, when heaven and earth pass away.

I read something else out of the disciples' image: their anxiety and concern that the house is not to be dusty and cold, comfortless and pitch dark, when the Lord returns. They do not want the master to see cobwebs which tell of neglect and resignation; they do not want the ice of cold calculation and petty self-concern to cover the walls and a mouldy smell of death to fill the air. Were that to happen the master's reactions would be unthinkable. Life in such a house of death would be unthinkable. Or would it? Isn't our world in some respects like a house of death? 'Watch', the disciples call to us. Live attentively! Let the spirit of hope blow through our Lord's house. Let the warmth of his love stream through his house, so that the mould of comfortlessness does not creep over the walls and a chill blast does not strike everyone icily in the face. Watch! For in every human being Christ the Lord, whose words do not pass away, is looking at you. And what are his words, if not the words of love, forgiveness and hope which he has given us? 'Love your neighbour as yourself.' 'Bless those who curse you.' 'All that you ask for in prayer you will receive, if only you believe.' These are words which he once again spelt out on the cross in his suffering and dying, 'Woman, behold your son,' he says to Mary in the Gospel of John, and to the Beloved Disciple, 'Behold your Mother.' In Luke he says, 'Father, forgive them, for they know not what they do,' and, 'Father, into your hands I commend my spirit.' Christ's words of love, forgiveness and hope – they remain beyond death, indeed beyond the end of the world. 'Heaven and earth will pass away, but my words will not pass away.' That is what we read in the text for today's sermon. That should give us comfort and support when life is comfortless and chaotic for us. 'My words – words of love, forgiveness and hope – will not pass away.' They are to be love and hope to us all our lives. They should help us to live more attentively and more perceptively. And may the peace of God which passes all our understanding keep our hearts and minds in Christ Jesus. Amen.

A sermon preached on 26 November 1989 in Coburg. For a description of the course of mourning see Y.Spiegel, *The Grief Process*.

4. Jesus and the limits of state power
A sermon on Matthew 22.15–22
(*Petra von Gemünden*)

The question of paying tax

Then the Pharisees went and took counsel how to entangle him in his talk. And they sent their disciples to him, along with the Herodians, saying, 'Teacher, we know that you are true, and teach the way of God truthfully, and care for no man; for you do not regard the position of men. Tell us, then, what you think. Is it lawful to pay taxes to Caesar, or not? But Jesus, aware of their malice, said, 'Why put me to the test, you hypocrites? Show me the money for the tax.' And they brought him a coin. And Jesus said to them, 'Whose likeness and inscription is this?' They said, 'Caesar's.' Then he said to them,

'Render to Caesar the things that are Caesar's, and to God the things that are
God's.' When they heard it, they marvelled, and they left him and went away.

'Render to Caesar the things that are Caesar's and to God the things
that are God's' – this short sentence has made history. Not just good
history, but also extremely problematical history. One could read of its
problematical effect last week in a local newspaper. It caused me
helpless grief, though I already knew the story. 'Handicapped Handed
Over to Nazi Murderers' – that was the headline. The article told how in
1940/41, within the framework of Hitler's 'merciful death' campaign,
hundreds of the mentally handicapped living in homes run by the
church were taken away and finally murdered. The rector of the church
organization responsible had issued instructions that the credentials of
those in charge of the transport were to be checked, but otherwise that
everything should be done to ensure that the move went as smoothly as
possible. In an article on the report, the journalist wrote: 'Rector
Lauerer resolved the dilemma between obeying an inhuman state and
the Christian command to love one's neighbour with a Lutheran
doctrine of the two kingdoms taken to extremes. He gave the state what
he thought was the state's and innocently preached mercy.' Here again
Jesus' saying 'Render to Caesar the things that are Caesar's and to God
the things that are God's' resounds. It has all too often made sorry
history – and yet I believe that this sorry history of its influence does not
match the intention of the saying. I am convinced that it is a liberating,
helpful gospel for life in our world. In search of its message I want to
invite you to make a journey with me to the time and world of Jesus, to
look more closely at the story of the tax money.

   The story takes place in Jerusalem, which is teeming with people, just
before Passover. These days are always very tense ones: it takes only a
tiny spark to set off a devastating fire. So the Romans are in a state of full
emergency. As a precaution, Pilate and his troops come to the Holy City
at this time of year. And now – perhaps in the temple forecourt, in the
shadow of the Antonia citadel, in which Pilate resides and where the
soldiers are billetted – there is that devious attempt to catch Jesus in a
trap and put him out of harm's way. To this end his opponents use the
most explosive political topic: the question of the hated poll tax.
Whereas our taxes are usually levied for the general welfare, the poll tax
at that time was in fact a tribute to the Roman occupying forces. This
tribute was exacted with the cruellest methods. We know this from the
Roman Lactantius, who writes: 'They tortured those eligible to pay tax

until they spoke out against themselves, and when pain had conquered, people wrote down taxable possessions which did not exist. No account was taken of age or state of health.'

We can easily imagine how high passions ran when it came to taxes. And now the Pharisees and Herodians came and asked Jesus, under the eyes of the temple police and the Roman legionaries, 'Tell us what you think. Is it right to pay tax to the emperor or not?' Unmistakably, the underlying question here was, 'What do you think of the Roman state?' The trap was obvious. If Jesus replied, 'Yes, one should pay taxes', then he would be seen as a traitor by the people; if he answered 'No', then he was a rebel who could easily be denounced to the Romans. But Jesus doesn't fall into the trap. He unmasks his questioners as hypocrites. 'Show me the money for paying tax,' he asks. And they give him a denarius. So they carry the money in their pockets. That shows that they have long since answered the question in their own lives. With his request 'Show me the money', Jesus turns their question against them and makes it an inquiry into their lives: 'At the point where you want to get at others, look first at yourselves and your lives.' And as though he had never seen a denarius before, Jesus asks, 'Whose likeness and inscription is this?' The question of the likeness is a question which shows up any Jews, because it immediately makes them think of the Second Commandment: 'You shall not make any image – either of what is in heaven above or on earth below, or in the water under the earth.'

And if we look more closely at the keystone of Jesus' argument, namely the denarius with Tiberius' image on it, we see his intention even more clearly. For on the denarius the emperor is depicted as an Olympian deity, and below his head is the inscription: Emperor Tiberius, the worshipful son of the divine Augustus. And on the other side of the denarius the dowager empress is enthroned as a goddess of peace. For any Jew that was an affront against the First Commandent and blasphemy. Jesus' criticism of the worship and divinization of the ruler can clearly be heard in his question, 'Whose likeness and inscription is this?' His adversaries can only quietly reply 'The emperor's.' So Jesus concludes, 'Give the emperor what is the emperor's'. And here that means: give the emperor back his blasphemous money. Give the tax money back to the one who minted it. But that is not all. For to 'Give the emperor what is the emperor's', Jesus adds unasked, 'And give to God what is God's.' That, in his view, is the all-important thing. 'Give God what is God's.' That may mean, 'Just reflect on what the coins of the emperor are. Nothing but minted silver. What is the image of the emperor? Nothing but the counterfeit of a mortal man fixed in metal. And by contrast, what is the image of the living, eternal God? In the very first book of the Bible it is written: that is what you are, that is what you and I are. Every human being is in God's image.'

The question whether or not we should pay tax to the emperor doesn't go far enough. The real question is: do you want to have yourself and your life stamped by dead gold and earthly power, which often enough stands on feet of clay and sometimes collapses with unexpected speed, as the prophet Daniel already wrote? Do you want to sell out your life to earthly success, to career and power, to yield to the pressures and demands of everyday life and run the risk of losing your soul in the process, of becoming hard and rigid in values which are dead, no matter how glittering they are? Is that what you really want? Or do you want to be the image of your creator, a mirror which seeks to reflect something of his devotion and love, his friendliness and his will for life? Do you want to tax your fellow human beings in accordance with status and power, their nationality and the colour of their skins, or do you want to seek the image of God in them? Only if you first seek God and God's image in men and women does the question about the emperor emerge in its true light.

That became clear to me once when I was doing practical work in a community in the hills of southern France. Ordinary people live there, mostly farmers, for whom the Bible is precious. Many generations ago, in the time of the Reformation, their ancestors had discovered the Bible as a liberating source of their life and had learned to read and write so that they could study it carefully. They were persecuted for their faith. But supported by the Bible, they acknowledged God alone as their Lord and stubbornly opposed the soldiers of the French king. They practised their worship secretly in remote valleys. Time and again they had to flee into the woods, and when they were captured, many preferred to go to the galleys or to prison than to abjure their faith in God and give up their Bible. And in this century, too, the descendants of those Protestants again lived out their personal interpretation of the commandment, 'Give to God what is God's.' At the risk of their lives, during the Third Reich they hid Jews in their homes, forged passes and ration books at the town hall, smuggled Jews by remote paths into Switzerland, and in so doing saved many lives. When an attempt was once made to compel the local pastor to betray the Jews and their hiding places, he simply replied. 'We don't know what a Jew is. We know only human beings.' Images of God.

These French Protestants illuminated for me the sentence: Only if you first seek God and God's image in human beings does the question about the emperor emerge in its true light.

Today we no longer live in the Third Reich. We have neither an emperor not a divine king. Our taxes are not exploitative payments of tribute to a foreign occupying power. I think that we must spell out the meaning of the sentence 'Give to the emperor what is the emperor's' afresh in each situation. Jesus' saying does not lay down what is the emperor's and what is God's. We must find out, each for ourselves, what that is, since situations change. But the guideline remains. God wants to shape our lives with his love. Every human being is God's creature – infinitely valuable and an image of the living God. An image of God, even if he or she is handicapped, as were the sick who were taken away to be killed. An image of God, even if he or she belongs to another people and another religion, like the Jews. An image of God, even if he or she is persecuted and seeks asylum among us. We Christians can freely object to inhuman ideas, since we are not bound here. We are independent of the enslaving powers of this world. Our dignity does not lie in outward recognition but in the image of the one who has created us and wants to be reflected in our life. Amen.

A sermon preached on 3 November 1991 in Coburg. For the historical and exegetical questions in this pericope cf. K.Wengst, *Pax Romana*.

5. Expecting God in the wilderness of life
A sermon on Luke 3.1–14
(*Gerd Theissen*)

In the fifteenth year of the reign of Tiberius Caesar, Pontius Pilate being governor of Judaea, and Herod being tetrarch of Galilee, and his brother Philip tetrarch of the region of Ituraea and Trachonitis, and Lysanias tetrarch of Abilene, in the high-priesthood of Annas and Caiaphas, the word of God came to John the son of Zechariah in the wilderness; and he went into all the region about the Jordan, preaching a baptism of repentance for the forgiveness of sins. As it is written in the book of the words of Isaiah the prophet, 'The voice of one crying in the wilderness: Prepare the way of the

Lord, make his paths straight. Every valley shall be filled, and every mountain and hill shall be brought low, and the crooked shall be made straight, and the rough ways shall be made smooth; and all flesh shall see the salvation of God.'

He said therefore to the multitudes that came out to be baptized by him, 'You brood of vipers, who warned you to flee from the wrath to come? Bear fruits that befit repentance, and do not begin to say to yourselves, "We have Abraham as our father"; for I tell you, God is able from these stones to raise up children to Abraham. Even now the axe is laid to the root of the trees; every tree therefore that does not bear good fruit is cut down and thrown into the fire.'

And the multitudes asked him, 'What then shall we do?' And he answered them, 'He who has two coats, let him share with him who has one; and he who has food, let him do likewise.' Tax collectors also came to be baptized, and said to him, 'Teacher, what shall we do?' and he said to them, 'Rob no one by violence or by false accusation, and be content with your wages.'

Advent is a time of expectation. In it the Bible becomes a textbook of expectation. It teaches us what we may expect in life, what is important to us. And it says that what is important to us in life is not this or that, but God. We expect too little if we do not wait on God. We do not yet have the right expectation if we do not notice that we dispense with God in the dark hours of our lives. We go wrong if we do not detect in joy that God's presence has touched us. But above all, we have illusions if we think that this expectation is without risk. On the contrary, it leads us into the wilderness – into a wilderness beyond life, beyond society, beyond our familiar self. The great teacher of this expectation is John the Baptist. He calls us into the wilderness in order to expect God there, and my task today will be to call your ideas and imaginations into the wilderness, on three excursions.

The first excursion takes us to the limits of life. I have seen the wilderness only once in my life, in Syria. Wherever one looks, there is sand, stones, an infinitely wide horizon, dead matter, eaten away by a burning wind, but with life hidden in it. When one returns to villages and cities, with greenery, human beings and houses, one becomes aware that our human world consists simply of small islands in a giant lifeless cosmos. But tremendous energy is invested in these islands. On the islands, the mosques in turn form yet smaller islands: places of coolness and clarity in the heat of the day. I love these mosques. With their strictness, simplicity and lack of imagery they remind me of the reformed churches which have been familiar to me since my childhood. I loved to sit on the floor in mosques and reflect. And it dawned on me that the people who worship God here constantly unite in their prayers with that tremendous energy which wills human life – life in the midst of the wilderness, life threatened by the wilderness. And they emanate the certainty that the Creator wants all this: the wilderness and life, and above all life in the wilderness and despite the wilderness.

Now in Syria I experienced not only the wilderness but for the first time in my life gun battles, minor political disturbances which probably never got into any news broadcasts. Sunnis were fighting Shi'ites and vice versa. It was uncanny. When the first shots were heard, people fled into the houses. The streets were empty in an instant. The tension could be felt in the city for a long time: in the tighter control by the army and the police. And I had a new theme to meditate on in the mosques: this tiny world in which we live is even more endangered from within than from outside – endangered by our inability to live together. By religious fanaticism. By nationalisms. By the mute repudiation of those who are different.

And I heard the voice of John the Baptist inside me. It said, 'Don't imagine that nothing could happen to you because you're descended from *homo sapiens*, and tower above other creatures because of your large brain. Perhaps you're only a dead branch on the tree of evolution. Perhaps soon it will have to be cut down, because it brings forth rotten fruit, because it has gone wrong. Isn't the axe already laid to the root of the tree? Why shouldn't creation begin all over again with pre-living structures? Why not develop new life from stones and dead matter?'

I don't find it difficult to imagine our relationship to the whole of reality in terms of the picture presented by John the Baptist. We live as if under the threat of harsh punishment: if we develop forms of life which go against the basic conditions of reality, if we do not convert in time – then a merciless judgment will strike us. John the Baptist and kindred apocalyptic seers saw that centuries ago in their visions – but they also put hope into their imagery: the hope that failure could be averted.

If one meditates like this on the edge of the wilderness – on the frontier between death and life – and affirms life as an island in a lifeless cosmos, then one has made a first basic decision: a decision for the experiment of human civilization – for risky life in the wilderness of the universe and despite this wilderness. And if it dawns on us when seeing people praying in mosques, synagogues and churches that this basic decision is the echo of a pre-existing decision for life – then God has come. Then God's will for creation has also grasped us. Then we have heard God's voice. Then what God expects from us becomes more important than anything that we have expected from God. But the voice says even more.

Here I must lure thoughts and imaginations for a second excursion into the wilderness. This time it is into the wilderness of Judaea, where John the Baptist is at work. He is a remarkable man, so remarkable that Luke omits the description of his exotic appearance which Mark gives us.

His clothing: camel hair and a leather girdle – a protest against those who wear fine clothes in the palaces of the rulers.

His food: locusts and wild honey – a protest against the kind of banquet celebrated by his ruler, Herod (though it should be added that some New Testament scholars think that locusts roasted in butter were a delicacy).

His abode: the wilderness, which in the Jordan valley looks comfortless, but which is broken by the Jordan and its narrow tributaries.

We all know such figures: sympathetic chaps with a beard, tartan shirt, Jesus sandals, organic food. Their very outfit conveys the message, 'You have the wrong life-style.' They put our life-style in question with gentle moral aggression.

Should we learn from John the Baptist to hear God's call in such outsiders? Should we wait for God there, with drop-outs on the edge of society? But how do we differ from drop-outs and demagogues? There were already such people then. There were prophets who promised signs and wonders in the wilderness and led many people astray. There was the Qumran community which referred to the same Isaiah text as John the Baptist did, 'In the wilderness prepare the way of the Lord', and who retreated from the wicked world to wait for the great battle at the end of days when all the children of darkness would be slain with their and God's help.

If Luke had had prophetic gifts, he could have foreseen yet other misleading figures: people with ties and good manners, who at the end of the twentieth century present to camera the message:

The voice of those in prosperity!
Shut up the way to our land,
that the others may remain in the wilderness.
Dig the trenches deep and make the barriers high,
that no one may get through to you
when fleeing persecution and threat.
Tell the immigration officials to keep them out

and the soldiers to track them down,
so that the whole human race can see
what a humane country we are,
we who guarantee asylum to anyone who is really persecuted –
in neighbouring countries.

Had Luke with prophetic foresight already known such deeply problematical words, he would have had one more reason for supplementing Mark's report about John the Baptist at a decisive point. Already in Mark, John applied to himself the saying of Isaiah.

The voice of one crying in the wilderness:
Prepare the way of the Lord,
make his paths straight.

Luke quotes this saying of Isaiah more fully. He adds:

Every valley shall be filled,
and every mountain and hill shall be brought low,
and the crooked shall be made straight,
and the rough ways shall be made smooth;
and all flesh shall see the salvation of God.

Luke breaks off the quotation at this point. For this is what is decisive for him – this is what distinguishes prophets from demagogues and other misleading voices. The salvation of which the true prophet speaks is that of the whole world. It applies to 'all flesh', i.e. to the whole human race. It applies not only to his own people, but to all peoples. Any prophet who promises salvation only for his own people – as opposed to the others, and to their detriment – is not a true prophet. God's salvation applies to all, or it is not God's salvtion.

Now one could say, 'That is true of God's salvation. We gladly share our religious faith with all people, but not our bread and butter. The salvation of which Luke speaks is spiritual salvation. It has nothing to do with politics and social equilibrium.'

One might even think that Luke foresaw such objections. For unlike Mark, he sets his account of John the Baptist in a political framework. He begins by dating John's appearance by five rulers and two church politicians. He mentions one after the other:
– the emperor Tiberius,
– Pontius Pilate the prefect of Judaea,
– Herod, the Roman client prince over Galilee,
– Philip, who ruled over parts of present-day Jordan,

– Lysanias, another client prince, ruling over part of present-day Lebanon.

And in addition, the two high-priests Annas and Caiaphas. The reader or hearer could hardly be told more clearly to pay attention, for now a figure was appearing who had something to do with politics.

In keeping with this, over and above Mark's account, Luke concludes by making John the Baptist call for practical consequences, the consequences of repentance:

– First, people are to share. Those who have two garments are to give one away. Similarly with their bread and butter.
– Secondly, the customs officers, who at that time collected not only tolls but taxes, are not to be corrupt.
– Thirdly, the soldiers (and in those days they were policemen at the same time) are not to plunder and extort.

In other words, those who have fiscal and military power are not to use it to exploit the weaker ones. Here we come up against politics once more: now not at the highest level but down below in the persons of customs officers and soldiers, in the persons of people who put domination into practice – the domination of the emperor Tiberius, Pontius Pilate, Herod.

Furthermore, Luke does not paint a positive picture of these rulers. He regards Herod as a rogue. For in a passage which comes shortly after our text, he writes: 'In addition to all the wicked things that Herod did, he had John put in prison.' We all know how that story ended.

So we are to go into the wilderness to this prophet, to wait for God. By that I understand that we are to distance ourselves from our society, from the distribution of opportunities in life that we all know about too well. As long as we live in our society, it seems normal to us. But if we look at our society from outside, from the perspective of the wilderness, then we can only regard with horror the great difference in opportunities – in our very own country between East and West, and even more between the developed nations and the rest of the world. No one has recipes for dealing effectively with such inequality in the world. But it would be cynical to accept them as inevitable, cynical to let hunger bite further, not just in Somalia but in many other places.

Here a second basic decision is required of us. The first was the decision for human culture generally. The second decision is made right in the midst of it: the decision for the weak and the disadvantaged. If we recognize that this decision, too, is just the echo of a greater will, then God has come among us. Then his concern for the poor and weak has grasped us, too. Then what God expects of us becomes more important than anything we expect of God. But his will requires yet more of us.

I want to direct your thoughts to the wilderness yet a third time, or more precisely to the Jordan, which runs right through the wilderness. That is where John the Baptist issues his summons to repentance, to baptism. He calls everyone to this. He calls everyone individually. He calls everyone to become different.

But can people become different? Here John the Baptist uses a bold metaphor which we no longer even recognize as such. He calls for fruits of repentance. He requires them of men and women, whom he compares with trees which are to be cut down if they bear no fruit. But how can a tree change? How can it bring forth better fruit? At another point the Bible is more sceptical about this. A good tree brings forth good fruit and a bad tree brings forth bad fruit. That's that. And that's how it will always be. Or have you ever seen a tree repent? Can it change its behaviour? John the Baptist challenges such scepticism. If God can make children out of stones, then God can also make new people out of old. And for that he offers baptism – as an ineradicable seal to indicate that we are born in order to be reborn. That we are not finished. That we can be and might be different.

John calls us into the wilderness to begin our life afresh there – where we leave behind the familiar roles; all the things that we have accumulated: our competence, our status, our firm expectations and also our confirmed disappointments. He calls us away from what we have become. Everyone pays a price for growing up. Recently I was browsing through notebooks I had filled with all kinds of deep thoughts between the ages of fifteen and twenty (reading them after thirty years called for a great deal of empathy towards oneself). In them I came upon a note which struck me: 'Become a character probably means throwing out nine of one's ten potential characters. One never becomes a character without loss.' We all have our junk rooms containing things that remain undeveloped – a bit of wilderness in ourselves. But we have to go into them if we are beginning again in the midst of life. A notion of God could be lying there which we still might think through to the end.

But perhaps I don't even need to lure you into this private wilderness. Perhaps you're already in the midst of it.

Perhaps illness has thrown your normal life out of joint.

Perhaps divorce has brought on a depression.

Perhaps an experience of injustice has hurt and disturbed you.

Perhaps you're aware that your best plans have failed.

Perhaps you despise yourself because you're no longer what you once wanted to be.

Perhaps you've reached the end of life, and with death comes the feeling, 'Was that all?'

In that case no one need summon you into the wilderness, because you are already in the midst of it.

If that is the case, hear the message of John the Baptist as consolation, as a voice in the midst of the wilderness of your life. There, in the wilderness, make ready the way of the Lord. He is coming there. He is looking for you there. And even if you think that the roots of your life are already withered and that everything is tottering, if you feel that the axe is already laid to them, even then, precisely then, the message of John the Baptist is for you: you can be free from the burden of the past, can become new. God is always ready to seek the new person in you. God is ready to take a small part of the new for the whole. God is ready to think through to a good end what went wrong in your life.

If that is the case, you have made a third basic decision. Not only a decision for a weak and questionable civilization in the wilderness of the universe, not only a decision for what is weak and questionable in this civilization, but a decision for what is weak and questionable in yourself. If you become aware that you are also engaged in bringing a greater will to its conclusion, then you are no longer a poor worm, but you are chosen to think God's thoughts to the end in your life. You are chosen to help to complete God's search for what is lost, including what is lost in you.

Advent is a time of expectation. In it we are called into the wilderness to expect God anew. We went in the expectation that God would make a way for our life. But he wants us to make a way for him. If we allow ourselves to be seized totally by this expectation, by his will for human life, for the weak among us and the weakness in us, then we are already preparing the way for God in this world, together with John the Baptist. John was a Jew. He was not a Christian. A Muslim could also have said everything that he did. So we should prepare the way for God in this world together with Muslims and Jews: together with them, together with John the Baptist, not against them. And if this way takes us through Nazareth, we shall welcome Jesus as our brother, as a brother who teaches us to live with other brothers and sisters in the Father's house –

also with Muslims and Jews: here at home and in Bosnia, in Syria, in Israel, and throughout the world.

And may the peace of God which surpasses all our understanding keep our hearts and minds in Christ Jesus. Amen.

A university sermon preached on 13 December 1992 in the Peterskirche, Heidelberg.

Bibliography

Ahn, B.-M., 'Jesus und das Minjung im Markusevangelium', in J.Moltmann (ed.), *Minjung. Theologie des Volkes Gottes in Südkorea*, Neukirchen-Vluyn 1984, 110–32

– , 'Das Subjekt der Geschichte im Markusevangelium', ibid., 134–69

Aland, B., 'Marcion/Marcioniten', *TRE* 22, 1992, 89–101

Albert, H., *Traktat über kritische Vernunft*, Tübingen 1968, [4]1980

Anderson, J.C. and Moore, S.D. (eds.), *Mark and Method. New Approaches in Biblical Studies*, Minneapolis 1992

Barth, H., and Schramm, T., *Selbsterfahrung mit der Bibel. Ein Schlüssel zum Leben und Verstehen*, Munich and Göttingen 1977

Barth, K., 'Menschenwort und Gotteswort in der christlichen Predigt', *ZZ* 3, 1925, 119–40 = F.Wintzer (ed.), *Predigt*, 95–116

– , 'Correspondence with Adolf von Harnack', in James M.Robinson (ed.), *The Beginnings of Dialectical Theology*, Richmond, Va. 1968, 165–90

– , *Church Dogmatics* IV.3.2, Edinburgh 1965

– , *Homiletik. Wesen und Vorbereitung der Predigt*, Zurich 1966

Benesch, H., *'Und wenn ich wüsste, dass morgen die Welt unterginge . . .' Zur Psychologie der Weltanschauungen*, Weinheim and Basel 1984

Berg, H.K., *Ein Wort wie Feuer. Wege lebendiger Bibelauslegung*, Munich and Stuttgart 1991

Berg, S., and Berg H.K., *Biblische Texte verfremdet* (12 vols.), Stuttgart and Munich 1986ff.

Berger, K., *Exegese des Neuen Testaments*, UTB 658, Stuttgart 1977, [2]1984

– , *Hermeneutik des Neuen Testaments*, Gütersloh 1988

– , *Historische Psychologie des Neuen Testaments*, SBS 146/7, Stuttgart 1991

Beutel, A., Drehsen, V., and Müller, H.M. (eds.), *Homiletisches Lesebuch. Texte zur heutigen Predigtlehre*, Tübingen 1986

Bohren, R., *Predigtlehre*, Munich 1971, [5]1986

Broich, U., and Pfister, M. (eds.), *Intertextualität. Formen, Funktionen, anglistische Fallstudien*, Tübingen 1986

Brox, N., *Falsche Verfasserangaben. Zur Erklärung der frühchristlichen Pseudepigraphie*, SBS 79, Stuttgart 1975

Bucher, A., *Bibel-Psychologie. Psychologische Zugänge zu den biblischen Texten*, Stuttgart, Berlin and Cologne 1992

Bultmann, R., 'New Testament and Mythology' (1941), in *New Testament and Mythology and Other Writings*, ed. Schubert M.Ogden, Philadelphia and London 1986, 1–44

Burrhoe, R.W., *Toward a Scientific Theology*, Belfast, Dublin and Ottawa 1981

Callan.T, *Psychological Perspectives on the Life of Paul. An Application of the Methodology of Gerd Theissen*, Lewiston, Queenston and Lampeter 1990

Cassirer, E., *Was ist der Mensch? Versuch einer Philosophie der menschlichen Kultur*, Stuttgart 1960

Crüsemann, F., *Die Tora. Theologie und Sozialgeschichte des alttestamentlichen Gesetzes*, Munich 1992

Dahm, K.-W., 'Hören und Verstehen. Kommunikationssoziologische Überlegungen zur gegenwärtigen Predigtnot', in id., *Beruf: Pfarrer. Empirische Aspekte zur Funktion von Kirche und Religion in unserer Gesellschaft*, Munich 1971, 218–44 = A.Beutel et al. (eds.), *Homiletisches Lesebuch*, 242–52

Daiber, K.F., *Predigt als religiöse Rede. Homiletische Überlegungen im Anschluss an eine empirische Untersuchung*, Predigen und Hören 3, Munich 1991

Dannowski, H.W., *Kompendium der Predigtlehre*, Gütersloh 1985

Das Buch Gottes. Elf Zugänge zur Bibel. Ein Votum des Theologischen Ausschusses der Arnoldshainer Konferenz, Neukirchen-Vluyn 1992

Davidson, O., *The Narrative Jesus. A Semiotic Reading of Mark's Gospel*, Aarhus 1993

Denecke, A., *Persönlich Predigen*, Gütersloh 1979

Dibelius, M., *From Tradition to Gospel*, reissued Cambridge, 1971

Dohmen, C., Jacob C., and Söding, T., *Neue Formen der Schriftauslegung*, QD 140, Freiburg, Basel and Vienna 1992

Drewermann, E., *Tiefenpsychologie und Exegese*, 1.2, Olten 1984/85

Eckstein, H.J., *Erfreuliche Nachricht – traurige Hörer? Gedanken zu einem ganzheitlichen Glauben*, Neuhausen and Stuttgart 1986

Egger, W., *Methodenlehre zum Neuen Testament. Einführung in linguistische und historisch-kritische Methoden*, Freiburg, Basel and Vienna

1987, [3]1993

Engemann, W., *Semiotische Homiletik*, THLI 5, Tübingen and Basel 1993

Fander, M., *Die Stellung der Frau im Markusevangelium. Unter besonderer Berücksichtigung kultur– und religionsgeschichtlicher Hintergründe*, MThA 8, Altenberge 1989

Fischer, H., (ed.), *Sprachwissen für Theologen*, Hamburg 1974

Fowler, R.M., 'Reader-Response Criticism: Figuring Mark's Reader', in J.C.Anderson and S.D.Moore (eds.), *Mark and Method*, 50–83

Fuchs, O., *Von Gott predigen*, Gütersloh 1984

Gemünden, P.von, *Vegetationsmetaphorik im Neuen Testament und in seiner Umwelt. Eine Bildfelduntersuchung*, NTOA 18, Fribourg and Göttingen 1993

–, 'Pflanzensymbolik', *TRE* (forthcoming)

Glebe-Moeller, J., *Politisk Dogmatik*, Aarhus 1982

Graf, F.W., and Tanner, K., 'Protestantische Staatsgesinnung. Zwischen Innerlichkeitsanarchie und Obrigkeitshörigkeit', *EvKom* 20, 1987, 699–704

Grözinger, A., *Praktische Theologie und Ästhetik*, Munich 1987, [2]1991

–, *Die Sprache des Menschen. Ein Handbuch. Grundwissen für Theologinnen und Theologen*, Munich 1991

Güttgemanns, E., *Offene Fragen zum Formgeschichte des Evangeliums*, BEvTh 54, Munich 1970

–, '"Generative Poetik" – Was ist das?', in H.Fischer (ed.), *Sprachwissen für Theologen*, Hamburg 1974, 97–113

Hallie, P.P., . . .*Dass nicht unschuldig Blut vergossen werde. Die Geschichte des Dorfes Le Chambon und wie dort gutes geschah*, Neukirchen-Vluyn 1983, [3]1990

Harnack, A. von, 'Fifteen Questions to Those Among the Theologians Who Are Contemptuous of the Scientific Theology', in James M.Robinson (ed.), *The Beginnings of Dialectical Theology*, Richmond, Va. 1968, 165–6

Hefner, P., *The Human Factor. Evolution, Culture and Religion in Theological Perspective*, Minneapolis 1993

Hessen, J., *Religionsphilosophie*, Vol.2, Munich and Basel [2]1955

Hezser, C., *Lohnmetaphorik und Arbeitswelt in Mt 20,1–16. Das Gleichnis von den Arbeitern im Weinberg im Rahmen rabbinischer Lohngleichnisse*, NTOA 15, Fribourg and Göttingen 1990

Hirschler, H., *Biblisch predigen*, Hanover [2]1988

Hochschild, R., *Sozialgeschichtliche Exegese. Zur Entwicklung, Geschichte und Methodik einer neutestamentlichen Forschungsrichtung*, Heidelberg theological dissertation, 1993 (forthcoming)

Hoffsümmer, W.M, *Kurzgeschichten. Kurzgeschichten für Gottesdienst, Schule und Gruppe* (4 vols.), Mainz 1981–91

Hollenweger, W.J., *Konflikt in Korinth/Memoiren eines alten Mannes. Zwei narrative Exegesen*, Munich 1978, ⁶1990

Hübner, K., *Kritik der wissenschaftlichen Vernunft*, Freiburg and Munich 1978, ³1986

Jaschke, H.-J., 'Irenäus von Lyon', *TRE* 16, 1987, 258–68

Jeanrond, W.G., *Text und Interpretation als Kategorien theologischen Denkens*, Tübingen 1986

– , *Theological Hermeneutics. Development and Significance*, New York 1991, reissued London 1994

Josuttis, M., 'Über der Predigtanfang', *MPTh* 53, 1964, 480ff. = *Rhetorik und Theologie*, 187–200

– , 'Über den Predigtaufbau', *MPTh* 54, 1965, 480ff. = *Rhetorik und Theologie*, 187–200

– , 'Der Prediger in der Predigt. Sündiger Mensch oder mündiger Zeuge?', in M.Josuttis, *Die Praxis des Evangeliums zwischen Politik und Religion*, Munich 1974, 70–94 (= F.Wintzer, ed., *Predigt*, 221–34, as extract)

– , *Rhetorik und Theologie in der Predigtarbeit. Homiletische Studien*, Munich 1985

– , 'Über den Predigtschluss', in *Rhetorik und Theologie*, 201–15

Jüttemann, G. (ed.), *Wegbereiter der Historischen Psychologie*, Munich and Weinheim 1988

Keller, C.A., 'Die Komplementarität von Leben und Tod im hinduistischen und im mesopotamischen Mythus', in G.Stephenson (ed.), *Leben und Tod in den Religionen. Symbol und Wirklichkeit*, Darmstadt 1985, 17–35

Langer, W. (ed.), *Handbuch der Bibelarbeit*, Munich 1985

Langer, S.K., *Philospohie auf neuem Wege. Das Symbol im Denken, im Ritus und in der Kunst*, Frankfurt 1965

Lapide, P., *Er predigte in ihren Synagogen. Jüdische Evangelienauslegung*, Gütersloh ⁴1984

Leiner, M., *Grundfragen einer textpsychologischen Exegese des Neuen Testaments*, Heidelberg theological dissertation 1993 (forthcoming)

Lips, H.von, *Weisheitliche Traditionen im Neuen Testament*, WMANT 64, Neukirchen 1990

– , 'Christus als Sophia. Weisheitliche Traditionen in der urchristlichen

Christologie', in *Anfänge der Christologie, FS F.Hahn*, Göttingen 1991, 75–95

Lübbe, H., 'Religion nach der Aufklärung' (1978), in W.Oelmüller, R.Dölle, J.Ebach, H.Przybylski (eds.), *Diskurs: Religion*, UTB 895, Paderborn, Munich, Vienna and Zurich 1979, ²1982, 315–33

– , *Religion nach der Aufklärung*, Graz, Vienna and Cologne 1986

Lüdemann, G., *Texte und Träume. Ein Gang durch das Markusevangelium in Auseinandersetzung mit Eugen Drewermann*, Bensheimer Hefte 71, Göttingen 1992

Luz, U. (ed.), *Zankapfel Bibel. Eine Bibel – viele Zugänge*, Zurich 1992

Luz, U., *Das Evangelium nach Matthäus*, EKK 1,1, Zurich and Neukirchen 1985

Mahlmann. T., 'Kritischer Rationalismus', *TRE* 20, 1990, 97–121

Martin, G.M. 'Predigt als "offenes Kunstwerk"? Zum Dialog zwischen Homiletik und Rezeptionsästhetik', *EvTh* 44, 1984, 46–58

–, 'Bibliodram', in W.Langer (ed.), *Handbuch der Bibelarbeit*, Munich 1987, 305–10

McFague, S., *Metaphorical Theology. Models of God in Religious Language*, Philadelphia and London 1982

– , *Models of God. Theology for an Ecological, Nuclear Age*, Philadelphia and London 1987

Meyer zu Uptrup, K., *Gestalthomiletik. Wie wir heute predigen können*, Stuttgart 1986

Mieth, D., 'Narrative Ethik', in id., *Moral und Erfahrung*, Fribourg 1977, 60–90

Mieth, I. and D., 'Vorbild oder Modell? Geschichten und Über-legungen zur narrativen Ethik', in G.Stachel and D.Mieth, *Ethisch handeln lernen*, Einsiedeln 1978, 106–16

Möller, C., *Seelsorglich predigen. Die parakletische Dimension von Predigt, Seelsorge und Gemeinde*, Göttingen 1983

Morgan, R. (with J.Barton), *Biblical Interpretation*, Oxford 1988

Müller, C.-R., and Siemen, H.-L., *Warum sie sterben mussten. Leidens-weg und Vernichtung von Behinderten aus den Neuendettelsauer Pflege-anstalten im 'Dritten Reich'*, Einzelarbeiten aus der Kirchen-geschichte Bayerns 66, Neustadt an dem Aisch 1991

Mussner, F., *Tractate on the Jews*, Philadelphia 1984

Niebergall, F., 'Eine "unmenschliche Theorie". Zu K.Fezer, Das Wort Gottes und die Predigt', *ChW* 42, 1928, 59–60 (= F.Wintzer, ed., *Predigt*, 122–4)

Noppen, J.P.van (ed.), *Erinnern, um Neues zu sagen. Die Bedeutung der*

Metapher für die religiöse Sprache, Frankfurt 1988

Osten-Sacken, P. von der, *Grundzüge einer Theologie im christlich-jüdischen Gespräch*, Munich 1982

Otto, G., *Grundlegung der Praktischen Theologie*, Munich 1986

– , *Handlungsfelder der Praktischen Theologie*, Munich 1988

Pfister, M., 'Konzepte der Intertextualität', in U.Broich and M.Pfister (eds.), *Intertextualität. Formen, Funktionen, anglistische Fallstudien*, Tübingen 1985, 1–30

Piper. H.C., 'Kommunikation und Kommunikationsstörungen in der Predigt', in F.Wintzer (ed.), *Predigt*, 235–44 (= H.C.Piper, *Predigtanalysen*, Göttingen 1976, 127–36)

Raguse, H., *Psychoanalyse und biblische Interpretation. Eine Auseinandersetzung mit Eugen Drewermanns Auslegung der Johannes-Apokalypse*, Stuttgart, Berlin and Cologne 1993

Ramsey, I.T., *Religious Language. An Empirical Placing of Theological Phrases*, London 1957, reissued 1982

Reich, H., 'Kann Denken im Komplementarität die religiöse Entwicklung im Erwachsenalter fördern? Überlegungen am Beispiel der Lehrformel von Chalkedon und weiterer theologischer Paradoxe', in M.Böhnke, K.H.Reich, L.Rivez (eds.), *Erwachsen im Glauben*, Stuttgart, Berlin and Cologne 1992, 127–54

Riches, J., *Jesus and the Transformation of Judaism*, London 1980

Ricoeur, P., *Hermeneutik und Strukturalismus: Der Konflikt der Interpretationen* I, Munich 1973

– , *Hermeneutik und Psychoanalyse: Der Konflikt der Interpretationen* II, Munich 1984

– , *Die Interpretation: Ein Versuch über Freud*, Frankfurt 1974

– , 'Philosophische und theologische Hermeneutik', in P.Ricoeur and E.Jüngel, *Metapher*, Munich 1974, 24–45

– , *Die lebendige Metapher*, Munich 1986

Riemann, F., 'Die Persönlichkeit des Predigers in tiefenpsychologischer Sicht', in R.Riess (ed.), *Perspektiven der Pastoralpsychologie*, Göttingen 1974, 152–66

Ritschl, D., 'Die Erfahrung der Wahrheit. Die Steuerung von Denken und Handeln durch implizite Axiome', in id., *Konzepte, Ökumene, Medizin, Ethik, Gesammelte Aufsätze*, Munich 1986, 147–66

Ritschl, D. and Jones, H.O., *'Story' als Rohmaterial der Theologie*, TEH 192, Munich 1976

Rössler, D., *Grundriss der Praktischen Theologie*, Berlin 1986

Sauter, G., *Was heisst nach Sinn fragen?*, Munich 1982

Schaeffler, R., *Fähigkeit zur Erfahrung. Zur transzendentalen Hermeneutik des Sprechens von Gott*, QD 94, Freiburg, Basel and Vienna 1982

Scharfenberg, J., and Kämpfer, H., *Mit Symbolen leben*, Olten 1980

Schottroff, L., 'Gewaltverzicht und Feindesliebe in der urchristlichen Jesustradition. Mt 5,38–48/Lk 6, 27–36', in *Jesus in Historie und Theologie. FS H.Conzelmann*, Tübingen 1975, 197–221 = *Befreiungserfahrungen*, 12–35

– , *Befreiungserfahrungen. Studien zur Sozialgeschichte des Neuen Testaments*, ThB 82, Munich 1990

Schottroff, L. and Stegemann, W., *Jesus von Nazareth – Hoffnung der Armen*, Stuttgart 1978, ²1981

– (ed.), *Der Gott der kleinen Leute. Sozialgeschichtliche Auslegungen* (2 vols.), Munich and Gelnhausen 1979

Schreuder, O., 'The Silent Majority', *Concilium* 111, 1978, 11–19

Schroer, H., 'Umberto Eco as Predigthelfer? Fragen an Gerhard Marcel Martin', *EvTh* 44, 1984, 58–63

Schulz von Thun, F., *Miteinander reden 1 – Störungen und Klärungen*, Reinbek bei Hamburg 19981

– , *Miteinander reden 2 – Stile, Werte und Persönlichkeitentwicklung*, Reinbek bei Hamburg 1989

Schüssler Fiorenza, E., *In Memory of Her. A Feminist Theological Reconstruction of Christian Origins*, Boston and London 1983

Schweitzer, A., *The Quest of the Historical Jesus*, London ³1950

Spaemann, R., 'Die Frage nach der Bedeutung de Wortes "Gott"', in id., *Einsprüche. Christliche Reden*, Einsiedeln 1977, 1–35

– , 'Über den Sinn des Leidens', ibid., 116–33

Sparn, W., *Leiden – Erfahrung und Denken. Materialen zum Theodizeeproblem*, ThB 67, Munich 1980

Spiegel, Y., *The Grief Process*, Nashville and London 1978

Stock, A., *Umgang mit theologischen Texten. Methoden, Analysen, Vorschläge*, Zurich, Einsiedeln and Cologne 1974

Stolz, F., *Grundzüge der Religionswissenschaft*, KVR 1527, Göttingen 1988

Struthers-Malbon, E., 'Narrative Criticism: How Does the Story Mean?', in J.C.Anderson and S.D.Moore, *Mark and Method*, 23–49

Sunden, H., *Gott erfahren. Das Rollenangebot der Religionen*, GTB 98, Gütersloh 1975

Theissen, G., *The Miracle Stories of the Earliest Christian Tradition*, Edinburgh and Philadelphia 1983

– , 'Synoptische Wundergeschichten im Lichte unseres Sprachverständnisses. Hermeneutische und didaktische Überlegungen', *WPKG* 65, 1976, 289–308

– , *On Having a Critical Faith*, London and Philadelphia 1977

– , *Psychological Aspects of Pauline Theology*, Edinburgh and Philadelphia 1987

– , *Biblical Faith. An Evolutionary Approach*, London and Philadelphia 1984

– , 'Evolutionäre Religionstheorie und biblische Hermeneutik', *WzM* 37, 1985,107–18

– , *The Shadow of the Galilean*, London and Philadelphia 1987

– , 'Aporien im Umgang mit den Antijudaismen des Neuen Testaments', in *Die Hebräische Bibel und ihre zweifache Nachgeschichte. FS R.Rendtorff*, Neukirchen 1990, 535–53

– , *The Open Door*, London and Minneapolis 1991

– , 'L'herméneutique biblique et la recherche de la vérité religieuse', *RThP* 122, 1990, 485–503 = P.Bühler and C.Karakash (eds), *Science et foi font système. Une approche herméneutique*, Lieux théologiques 21, Geneva 1992, 135–54

– , 'Die Bibel an der Schwelle des dritten Jahrtausend. Überlegungen zu einer Bibel-didaktik für das Jahr 1992', *ThPr* 27, 1992, 4–23

– , 'Identité et expérience de l'angoisse dans le Christianisme primitif. Une contribution à la psychologie de la religion des premiers chrétiens', *ETR* 68, 1993, 161–83

– , 'Sociological Research into the New Testament. Some Ideas Offered by the Sociology of Knowledge for a New Exegetical Approach', in id., *Social Reality and the Early Christians*, Minneapolis 1993, 1–29

– , 'Methodenkonkurrenz und hermeneutischer Konflikt. Pluralismus in Exegese und Lektüre der Bibel', in *Pluralismus und Identität, VIII. Europäischer Theologenkongress Wien 1993*, Gütersloh 1995

– , *Lichtspuren. Predigten und Bibelarbeiten*, Gütersloh 1994

Theissen, G., et al., *Le défi homilétique. Exégèse au service de la prédication*, Geneva 1994

Tholuck, A., 'Einige Worte über die Predigt für die Gebildeten in unseren Tagen. Vorrede zur 2.Sammlung der Predigten' (1835), in F.Wintzer, ed., *Predigt*, 58–66

Thurneysen, E., 'Die Aufgabe der Predigt' (1921), in id., *Das Wort Gottes und die Kirche*, ThB 44, Munich 1971, 95–106 (extract in F.Wintzer, ed., *Predigt*, 117–21)

Tillich, P., *Systematic Theology* I, Chicago 1951 reissued London 1978

Trobisch, D., *Die Entstehung der Paulusbriefsammlung. Studien zu den Anfängen christliche Publizistik*, NTOA 10, Fribourg and Göttingen 1993

Vogt, T., *Angst und Identität im Markusevangelium. Ein text-psychologischer und sozialgeschichtlicher Beitrag*, NTOA 26, Freiburg and Göttingen 1993

Watson, F. (ed.), *The Open Text. New Directions for Biblical Studies?*, London 1993

Welker, M., *Gottes Geist. Theologie des Heiligen Geistes*, Neukirchen-Vluyn 1992

Wengst, K., *Pax Romana and the Peace of Jesus Christ*, London 1987

Wink, W., *Transforming Bible Study*, London and Nashville 1981

Wintzer, F. (ed.), *Predigt. Texte zum Verständnis und zur Praxis der Predigt in der Neuzeit*, ThB 80, Munich 1989

Notes

Books and articles listed in the bibliography are quoted by author and short title only.

Preface

   1. G.Theissen et al., *Le défi homilétique.*

Introduction: Dimensions of Preaching

   1. The move towards a new understanding of the process of tradition was introduced in New Testament exegesis by Güttgemanns, *Offene Fragen.* There is a good summary of his programme in id., '"Generative Poetik" – Was ist das?'. Cf. also Stock, *Umgang mit theologischen Texten.*
   2. The priority of the world of the text over the subjective intention of the author and the decision of the reader has been worked out in particular by P.Ricoeur, cf. e.g. 'Philosophische und theologische Hermeneutik'.
   3. I have attempted to demonstrate this by means of the transmission of miracle stories: Theissen, *Miracle Stories.*
   4. Cf. Broich and Pfister (eds.), *Intertextualität*; cf. especially Pfister, 'Konzepte der Intertextualität', 1–30.
   5. Cf. Theissen, 'Synoptische Wundergeschichte', 298f.
   6. For what follows cf. Engemann, *Semiotische Homiletik.* Engemann analyses sermons in terms of the relationships between significant, significate and referent. The semiotic insight that signs gain their significance within a sign system (a langue) is irrelevant for him. The ideas derived from his homiletics which are presented here differ, despite the related semiotic approach.
   7. For the 'open text' cf. Martin, 'Predigt als "offenes Kunstwerk"?'. See Schroer, 'Umberto Eco als Predigthelfer?'. In exegesis the concept (not the substance) has in my view emerged only recently; cf. Watson (ed.), *The Open Text* (not available to me in time). For the substance cf. already Berger, *Exegese des Neuen Testaments*, 92ff.
   8. Cf. the theoretical religious reflections on the topic 'religion and change' in Riches, *Jesus and the Transformation of Judaism*, 20–45: religious innovation takes place when concepts and ideas acquire new connotations. So they are

not as yet metaphors. A metaphor combines two denotations which according to conventional rules do not belong together.

9. Cf. the definition of Keller, 'Die Komplementarität von Leben und Tod', 137–35. He defines 'a system of religion as a comprehensive, multi-dimensional sign-system which makes communication possible between a religious community and the supreme, ultimately valid realities which prove to be at work in it' (19). This definition goes with the cultural-linguistic theories of religion – as distinct from expressive and cognitive theories which regard religion as an expression of experiences or as a world of ideas. Here religion is regarded as a system of signs rather than symbols because 'symbols' are specific forms of very complex signs.

10. Cf. Cassirer, *Was ist der Mensch?*; Langer, *Philosophie auf neuem Wege*.

11. This statement is very 'Protestant': in Protestantism scripture is regarded as a decisive and sufficient basis of Christian faith (*sola scriptura*). *De facto*, however, traditions and customs have constantly been added to it.

12. Rössler, *Grundriss der Praktischen Theologie*, 345.

13. Ritschl, 'Die Erfahrung der Wahrheit'. For the discussion of this approach cf. W.Huber, E.Petzold and T.Sundermeier (eds.), *Implizite Axiome. Tiefenstrukturen des Denkens und Handelns*, Munich 1990.

14. Cf. von Lips, *Weisheitliche Traditionen im Neuen Testament*; id., 'Christus als Sophia'.

I. Preaching as an Opportunity to Actualize the Biblical World of Signs

1. Cf. Trobisch, *Die Entstehung der Paulusbriefsammlung*.

2. Cf. the subtitle of my collection of sermons *The Open Door. Variations on Biblical Themes*.

3. The following sketch of basic motifs already appeared in a slightly different form in my 'Die Bibel an der Schwelle der dritten Jahrtausend'.

4. It is not even desirable that they should ever be finally formulated. In preparing a sermon, the preacher should reckon with the possibility that she or he will constantly discover new basic motifs arising from the concrete text.

5. Bohren, in his impressive *Homiletik. Predigtlehre*, has stated that the Spirit is the fundamental presupposition of preaching, and rightly so. The 'spirit' is communicated through the letters of the Bible without being identical with its texts. To be grasped by this spirit, i.e. at least to have internalized some basic biblical motifs, so that one perceives God, the world and life in its light, is the decisive presupposition of preaching. Such an internalization of basic biblical motifs takes place in disclosure situations which are beyond our control. They cannot be planned methodically, but they can be reflected on hermeneutically. I am aware that my reflections on 'the theory of signs' in connection with homiletics is often in tension with the consistent development of dialectical theology in Bohren's book. For that very reason I would like to draw attention to what we have in common.

6. Thus sermons about 'images' should not be excluded. 'The symbolic language of faith' comprises not only texts but also substantive pictures. However, I cannot imagine a sermon only about images in which biblical motifs appear. It would be something different to illustrate or alienate a biblical text with the help of images. But in that case the sermon would not be 'about' these images but about texts with the help of images.

7. Cf. Stolz, *Grundzüge der Religionswissenschaft*, 101ff.

8. For metaphor cf. Ricoeur, *Die lebendige Metapher*; Noppen (ed.), *Erinnern, um Neues zu sagen*; Grözinger, *Die Sprache des Menschen*, 94–129.

9. Cf. von Gemünden, *Vegetationsmetaphorik im Neuen Testament*.

10. This is a finding by P.von Gemünden (see n.9); cf. also her forthcoming article 'Pflanzensymbolik'.

11. This field of images is investigated by Hezser, *Lohnmetaphorik und Arbeitswelt*.

12. Cf. also the variation of the house metaphor in the sermon by Petra von Gemünden on Mark 13.31–37 (sermon 4 below). The metaphor of the house is used to depict the process of mourning and restructured cognitively; the forsaken house becomes an expectant house.

13. The deliberate re-metaphorization of a conventional metaphor in which we are no longer aware of the semantic tension between image and substance (or the one who provides the image and the one who receives it) is also fruitful for hermeneutics. In the text above I have provoked such a re-metaphorization by a literal misunderstanding of the metaphor 'fruits of repentance': trees cannot 'repent' – they remain in the same place, nor can human beings who repent produce 'fruits' in the literal sense.

14. For the distinction between metaphor and symbol cf. von Gemünden, *Vegetationsmetaphorik*, 19ff.

15. Cf. the variation on the wilderness symbolism in my sermon on Luke 3.1–14 (example 5 below).

16. I think that I read this interpretation in C.G.Jung, but I cannot identify where.

17. Cf. Grözinger, *Sprache*, 164ff.

18. Cf. the retelling of Acts 10.1–35 by Petra von Gemünden (example 1). I have adopted various fictitious perspectives, for example in 'Believing and Thanking. On the Gift of Changing Good Fortune into Gratitude (Luke 17.11–19)', in *The Open Door*, 94–101.

19. I have presented this 'reformulation' of John 8.43–44 in 'Aporien im Umgang mit den Antijudaismen des Neuen Testaments'.

20. Cf. the sermon by Petra von Gemünden on Matt.22.15–22 (sermon 3 below).

21. One example is the variation of the action in 'The Lost Sheep, or God's Remarkable Mathematics' (Luke 15.3–7), in *The Open Door*, 95–101.

22. We in fact find statements which come near to 'love of the enemy' even in the mouths of rulers and the powerful. Seneca, for a time one of the most

powerful men in the Roman empire, quotes the following maxims in *de benef.* IV, 26, 1: 'If you imitate the gods, it is said, then also do good deeds to ungrateful men; for the sun also rises on criminals and the seas are also open to pirates.' For the social context of such maxims see Schottroff, 'Gewaltverzicht und Feindesliebe'.

23. Cf. 'Letters to Exiles. Variations on the Letter of Jeremiah (Jer.29.1, 4–14)', in *The Open Door*, 24–32.

24. Cf. the well-known saying of Karl Barth's: 'Preaching has to speak out of the Bible, but not concerning it', *Church Dogmatics* IV.3.2, 869.

25. The distinction between basic biblical motifs and texts, between spirit and letter, can help us to understand why with a clear conscience preachers sometimes preach against a biblical text. They know that the spirit of the Bible gives them the freedom to criticize the letter.

II. *Preaching as an Opportunity to Develop the Open Text*

1. Cf. Bohren, *Predigtlehre*, 149: 'Since exegesis is in deep crisis and tendencies are becoming evident in homiletics to break the primacy of exegesis, it will be necessary to emphasize the usefulness of exegesis for preaching.'

2. Cf. the account given on the basis of personal experience by Meyer zu Uptrup, *Gestalthomiletik*. However, the 'scope method' was controversial. No less a figure than Karl Barth wrote polemic against it, cf. id., *Homiletik. Wesen und Vorbereitung der Predigt*, Zurich 1966 (a transcription of a Bonn seminar on homiletics in the winter semester of 1932 and the summer semester of 1933), 34f.; 'If God is willing to speak only in preaching, neither scheme nor scope may get in the way' (34).

3. Cf. Bohren, *Predigtlehre*, 148: 'If exegesis preserves the preacher from being led astray by the public, it prevents the preacher from allowing himself to be guided by the results of religious market research.'

4. Hirschler, *Biblisch predigen*.

5. There is a masterly survey of the development of biblical exegesis extending as far as the linguistic and sociological approaches by R.Morgan (with J.Barton), *Biblical Interpretation*. Further introductions with new exegetical approaches include Berger, *Exegese des Neuen Testaments*; Berg, *Ein Wort wie Feuer*; Anderson and Moore (eds.), *Mark and Method*. Since 1993 the journal *Biblical Interpretation. A Journal of Contemporary Approaches*, which is particularly open to new approaches, has been published by E.J.Brill, Leiden.

6. Cf. Jüttemann (ed.), *Wegbereiter der historischen Psychologie*.

7. Luz, *Das Evangelium nach Matthäus*, 78–82, offers a good introduction to the enterprise stimulated by H.G.Gadamer's hermeneutics to integrate the history of the influence of texts into their exegesis. This commentary implements the programme in a convincing way.

8. Jeanrond, *Text und Interpretation*, 104ff.; id. *Theological Hermeneutics*, 93–

119, offers a brief account.

9. Cf. Ricoeur, 'Philosophische und theologische Hermeneutik', 24ff.

10. Leiner, *Grundfragen einer textpsychologischen Exegese des Neuen Testaments*, 3ff.

11. Ibid., 219ff.

12. Ibid., 130–52.

13. Here I am following K.Hübner, *Kritik der wissenschaftlichen Vernunft*, 404ff.

14. With Berger, *Hermeneutik des Neuen Testaments*, 108ff., I would argue for a distinction between exegesis and application.

15. Here I am following Jeanrond, *Text and Interpretation*, 66ff., 119f.; id., *Theological Hermeneutics*, 116ff.

16. In what follows I am picking up notions from my 'Methodenkonkurrenz und hermeneutischer Konflikt'.

17. Text-critical approaches comprise a wealth of methodological innovations. Their common feature is that they are all inspired by linguistics. A scientific survey is given by Berger, *Exegese des Neuen Testaments*, 1977; Egger, *Methodenlehre zum Neuen Testament*, offers an introduction to exegetical methodology on a textual linguistic basis. Davidson, *The Narrative Jesus*, provides a structuralist-semiotic methodology.

18. Cf. Struthers-Malbon, 'Narrative Criticism: How does the Story Mean?'; Fowler, 'Reader-Response Criticism: Figuring Mark's Reader'.

19. For the Gospel of Mark, see Vogt, *Angst und Identität im Markusevangelium*.

20. Hochschild, *Geschichte der sozialgeschichtlichen Exegese*, offers a survey and stocktaking of sociological exegesis.

21. In Germany social-kerygmatic exegesis has been impressively presented by L.Schottroff; cf. ead., *Befreiungserfahrungen*; with Stegemann, *Jesus von Nazareth – Hoffnung der Armen*. Cf. also Schottroff and Stegemann (eds.), *Der Gott der kleinen Leute*.

22. Cf. Theissen, *Psychological Aspects of Pauline Theology*; Berger, *Historische Psychologie des Neuen Testaments*; Bucher, *Bibel-Psychologie*. Leiner, *Grundfragen einer textpsychologischen Exegese des Neuen Testaments*, is a basic study. Vogt, *Angst und Identität im Markusevangelium*, offers a psychological exegesis.

23. Drewermann, *Tiefenpsychologie und Exegese*, I.2. There is criticism of his programme by, among others, Lüdemann, *Texte und Träume*; Raguse, *Psychoanalyse und biblische Interpretation*. Callan, *Psychological Perspectives on the Life of Paul*, offers an alternative psychoanalytical methodology.

24. The great theme of Ricoeur's hermeneutics is the conflict of interpretations: cf. id., *Hermeneutik und Strukturalismus*; *Hermeneutik und Psychoanalyse*. He discusses this conflict of interpretation above all by means of psychoanalysis in *Die Interpretation: Ein Versuch über Freud*.

25. This is not the place to discuss sociological and psychological criticism of religion. Cf. my attempt in *Arguments for a Critical Faith*.

26. Leiner, *Grundfragen einer textpsychologischen Exegese*, 86ff., 153ff., shows that the tendencies in psychology which are problematical for its theological reception are themselves resisted in psychology, namely: '1. psychologism, in so far as it represents the comprehensive claim of a single discipline and claims to destroy the claim to valid knowledge; 2. determinism, in so far as it rejects human freedom; 3. objectivism, in so far as it denies that individual and subjective experience is outside our control and cannot be repeated in language; 4. dualism, in so far as it rejects the unity of the human being; and 5. a failure to note the historicity of experience and behaviour' (87).

27. For Jewish-Christian reading of the Bible see the journal *Kirche und Israel, Neukirchener Theologische Zeitschrift*, which has been appearing since 1986. As summaries cf. also Mussner, *Tractate on the Jews*, and von den Osten-Sacken, *Theologie*.

28. In addition to the representatives of a social-kerygmatic exegesis in Germany listed in n.21, mention should also be made of the 'material exegesis' which has arisen in the Romance countries, and 'Latin American' exegesis. Cf. Berg, *Ein Wort wie Feuer*, 227–49, 373–300. In addition there is the Korean Minjung theology, the exegesis of which is represented by B.-M.Ahn; cf. id., 'Jesus und das Minjung im Markusevangelium', and 'Das Subjeckt der Geschichte im Markusevangelium'.

29. Cf. Berg, *Ein Wort wie Feuer*, 250–72. Schüssler Fiorenza, *In Memory of Her*, provides a summary. One work which I find convincing is Fander, *Die Stellung der Frau im Markusevangelium*.

30. Cf. von Harnack, 'Fifteen Questions', and Barth's response, in *The Beginnings of Dialectical Theology*.

31. Cf. Dibelius, *From Tradition to Gospel*, 8–34.

32. Cf. Bultmann, 'New Testament and Mythology'.

33. Both approaches are rightly distinguished and brought into a dialogue with other approaches in Luz (ed.), *Zankapfel Bibel*.

34. Cf. Dannowski, *Kompendium der Predigtlehre*, 17f. For the mediating form of alienation see Berg, *Ein Wort wie Feuer*, 366–85. There are valuable suggestions in Berg and Berg, *Biblische Texte verfremdet*.

35. Cf. Berg, *Ein Wort wie Feuer*, 167–95. The term is particularly associated with Wink, *Transforming Bible Study*, a combination of archetypal psychological exegesis and historical-critical method and group work. Barth and Schramm, *Selbsterfarhung mit der Bibel*, is more open in its choice of psychoological approach. It is good that here professional exegetes are adopting new forms of practical exegesis, in which, rightly, not only the text but also the reader is 'expounded', and in a group situation.

36. Cf. Martin, 'Bibliodrama'.

37. Cf. the brief account in *Das Buch Gottes*, 120–34. The best-known representative of this is Hollenweger, *Konflikt in Korinth*. My book *The Shadow of the Galilean* is also 'narrative exegesis'.

38. Cf. Berg and Berg, *Biblische Texte verfremdet*.

39. Cf. the 'Obstinate Prophecy. A Christmas Sermon on Isaiah 7.10–16', in *The Open Door*, 1–23.

40. Cf. 'On Changing Human Beings and the World. A Bible Study on Mark 13.28–37; Luke 13.6–9', in *The Open Door*, 67–78.

41. Cf. 'Cain and Abel. A Murder Trial Revisited (Genesis 4.1–16)', in *The Open Door*, 1–9.

42. Cf. 'Ist die Kritik des Paulus am Gesetz antijüdisch? Eine Predigt zum Israelsonntag (Röm.9,1–5. 9,30–10,4)', in *Lichtspuren*, 167–74.

43. 'Mourning at a Loss Faced with Mass Graves. A Sermon for a National Day of Mourning (Rom.8.19–27)', in *The Open Door*, 145–51.

44. Cf. the lower Rhineland maxim, 'The worst suffering is what people do to themselves', in ' "Ihr seid kein Dreck, ihr seid Samen!" Von der Weisheit meiner Grossmutter (Lukas 8, 4–8)', in *Lichtspuren*, 139–46.

III. Preaching as an Opportunity to Enter into Dialogue with God

1. Benesch, *'Und wenn ich wüsste, dass morgen die Welt unterginge . . .'*, 17ff., gives a very impressive description of the reasons why we defend our intimate spiritual sphere.

2. The making of contact between God and human beings can be described from two sides: both sides seek this contact. Karl Barth understands preaching as the 'service of the church' to the word of God and defines it from two perspectives: 1. 'This service . . . can only consist in creating attentiveness, respect and objective understanding of God's own word'; and 2. 'Preaching is addressed to the human being who has to ask for God and can only ask for God' ('Menschenwort und Gotteswort in der christlichen Predigt', 103, 106).

3. In my view it is incorrect to see the historical context of 'dialectical theology' as an anti-modernist revival movement. The struggle over the autonomy of religion is a modern feature; however, it is not only to be found in the dialectical theologians. In homiletics, dialectical theology leads to one sided concepts. Engemann, *Semiotische Homiletik*, 142ff., has rightly criticized it as a threefold homiletic mythology of the indispensability of the preacher, the independence of the message and the irresponsibilty of the hearer. However, precisely from a semiotic standpoint one has to concede that talk of the Word of God establishing itself does make sense if one regards religion as a self-organizing system of signs in which an autonomous centre is to define everything. The 'Word of God' can be taken as such an autonomous centre. However, this should not distract our attention from the fact that sign-systems are shaped by the interpretative activity of human beings and that they are 'open systems' which are involved in an interaction with the world around.

4. Barth, *Homiletik*, goes beyond such a 'hope' when he defines preaching in two ways: 1. as the Word of God, and 2. as the interpretation of the text as 'an

announcement of what they (viz. human beings) have to hear from God himself' (30). An announcement is far more than a hope – even if the announcement refers not to what people will hear but what they should hear.

5. If it is necessary in hermeneutics to make a distinction between understanding and agreement, it is similarly appropriate in homiletics to distinguish between a 'successful' and an 'influential' sermon. Cf. Dannowski, *Kompendium der Predigtlehre*, 124: 'A sermon is successful when the congregation has understood what the preacher is concerned about . . . A communication is influential when the congregation also affirms this inwardly.'

6. Here I am following the ideas of Grözinger, *Praktische Theologie und Ästhetik*.

7. For the question of theodicy cf. Sparn, *Leiden – Erfahrung und Denken*. Religion is working on the question of theodicy, but it does not offer any intellectual solution. Lübbe, *Religion nach der Aufklärung*, 195–206, claims, probably rightly, that if one could solve the question of theodicy with a theoretical arugment, religion would become superfluous as a way of coping with contingency.

8. Spaemann, 'Die Frage nach der Bedeutung des Wortes "Gott" '. With this definition of the concept of God Spaemann stands in an older tradition which defines the 'holy' as a unity of reality and value. Cf. Hessen, *Religionsphilosophie* 2, 96ff.

9. This 'definition' is deliberately as wide as it is so that it can embrace very different concepts of God. Tillich's understanding of God, expressed in his *Systematic Theology*, Vol.1, is governed by two formal criteria of theological statements: 1. 'Only those propositions are theological which deal with their object in so far as it can become a matter of ultimate concern for us' (12). 2. 'Only those statements are theological which deal with their object in so far as it can become a matter of being or not-being for us' (14). Granted, Tillich constantly asserts that God is Being itself. But *de facto* he has already always attached meaning and value to this Being itself. This tension is included in any 'more naive' understanding of God. In the language of traditional biblical theology, God is thought of e.g. a creator and redeemer.

10. I know the objections made by Sauter, *Was heisst nach Sinn fragen?*, to a theological use of the concept of meaning. Can the meaning of action and the meaning of a text be transferred to contexts which derive neither from human action or human speech? However, does not his conclusion contain precisely this transference: a legitimate theological question about meaning is shaped by a knowing ignorance, 'by a knowledge that the world does not circle dumbly on itself but that in it can be perceived that which supports and sustains it, the creative activity of God' (169).

11. Cf. Theissen, 'L'herméneutique biblique et la recherche de la vérité religieuse'.

12. Cf. Albert, *Traktat über kritische Vernunft*; Mahlmann, 'Kritischer

Rationalismus', *TRE* 20, 1990, 97–121, esp.105.

13. Cf. Ramsey, *Religious Language*, 'disclosure situations'.

14. Thus Lübbe, 'Religion ist "Kultur des Verhaltens zum Unverfügbaren"', 324.

15. For this restructuring of experience cf. especially Sunden, *Gott erfahren*, and ch.2 on 'faith as illuminated by psychology and theology' (29–58).

16. Cf. above all McFague, *Metaphorical Theology*; ead., *Models of God*. In this book she develops three metaphors as new models of God: God as mother, lover and friend.

17. Cf. example 5 below.

18. Cf. 'Ist die Kritik des Paulus am Gesetz antijüdisch? Eine Predigt zum Israel-Sonntag', in *Lichtspuren*, 167–74.

19. Cf. '"Wir Menschen sollten mehr als Affen sein!" Eine antiautoritäre Predigt (Mark 10.35–45)', in *Lichtspuren*, 132–8.

20. Meyer zu Uptrup, *Gestalthomiletik*, 135ff., offers a systematic discussion of the homiletic use of narrative texts and structures.

21. Cf. Hoffsümmer, *Kurzgeschichten*.

22. Cf. Reich, 'Kann Denken im Komplementarität die religiöse Entwicklung im Erwachsenenalter fördern?', esp. 147f. on the problem of theodicy.

23. Aland, 'Marcion/Marcioniten'. Of course the God of the Old Testament is in himself a 'synthesis' of being and meaning. For justice is a value. But he sees above all to the actual form of the world.

24. Jaschke, 'Irenäus von Lyon'.

25. I have taken over the term from Graf and Tanner, 'Protestantische Staatsgesinnung'. However, the authors demonstrate the tendency towards internal anarchy not by means of the doctrine of the law but by means of the doctrine of two kingdoms.

26. Cf. Crüsemann, *Die Tora*.

27. Cf. Ritschl and Jones, *'Story' als Rohmaterial der Theologie*.

28. One concern of Fuchs, *Von Gott predigen*, is to restore the 'indicative of the good news' (9) in place of the strong ethical accent of many sermons. He therefore entitles his reflections on preaching 'reflections on an indicative homiletic' (9ff.).

29. Cf. Spaemann, 'Über den Sinn des Leidens'.

30. Among the sermon examples below there are two which are completely dominated by the conflict between reality and value; Petra von Gemünden's sermon on Matt.25.31–40 for a national day of mourning (example 2) shows this conflict in social experience, while that for the commemoration of the dead, on Mark 13.31–37 (sermon 4), is governed by the individual experience of death and mourning.

IV. Preaching as an Opportunity to Communicate an Orientation for Life

1. I have attempted to interpret religious experience as an experience of resonance and absurdity in my *On Having a Critical Faith*.

2. Cf. R.Schaeffler, *Fähigkeit zur Erfahrung*.

3. As every sermon seeks both to confirm basic motifs and 'create' or recreate them in the hearer, one cannot make a distinction between 'edifying' and 'revivalist' sermons in actual worship.

4. Cf. Bultmann, 'New Testament and Mythology'.

5. Ricoeur, 'Philosophische und theologische Hermeneutik', 41, distinguishes cosmic aspects, social and historical-cultural aspects and personal aspects in the 'world of the Bible'.

6. It lost 'control of the picture of the world', as H.Lübbe, *Religion nach der Aufklärung*, Graz, Vienna and Cologne 1986, 10ff., puts it.

7. I have already sketched out the following ideas (including the parable) in 'Kunst als Zeichensprache des Glaubens', in *Lichtspuren*, 203–19, esp.204ff.

8. Cf. Benesch, *'Und wenn ich wüsste . . .'*, 22ff.

9. It seems to me more promising to take up the suggestions of R.W.Burrhoe, *Toward a Scientific Theology*, Belfast, Dublin and Ottawa 1981, as is done by the group centred on the American journal *Zygon*. Cf. now P.Hefner, *The Human Factor. Evolution, Culture and Religion in Theological Perspective*, Minneapolis 1993.

10. Cf. Theissen, *Biblical Faith*; id., 'Evolutionäre Religionstheorie und biblische Hermeneutik'.

11. The sermon by Petra von Gemünden on the pericope about paying tax, Matt.22.15–22 (sermon 4 below), can serve as an instance of a political sermon in which sociological insights are activated for the application. Paying tax does not have the same function now that it did then. But recourse to the image of God in human beings in the face of any power which absolutizes itself is as topical now as then.

12. Cf. Mieth, 'Narrative Ethik'; Mieth and Mieth, 'Vorbild oder Modell? Geschichten und Überlegungen zur narrativen Ethik'.

13. Hochschild, *Sozialgeschichtliche Exegese*, 1993, offers a good survey of sociological research from the nineteenth century to the present day. I offer a brief survey in my 'Sociological Research into the New Testament'.

14. Cf. Lübbe, *Religion nach der Aufklärung*, 127ff.

15. Drewermann, *Tiefenpsychologie und Exegese*. Doubtless Drewermann's meditations – I would not call them exegesis – are of great practical value. He can bring biblical texts to life again for pastoral work, instruction and preaching. But he does not bring out every aspect.

16. Cf. Theissen, 'Identité et expérience de l'angoisse dans le christianisme primitif'; Vogt, *Angstbefähigung und Identitätsbildung im Markusevangelium*.

17. Cf. Berger, *Historische Psychologie des Neuen Testaments*, 1991. My

reflections on this can be found in *Psychological Aspects of Pauline Theology*. Here once again I would refer to Leiner, *Grundfragen textpsychologischer Exegese*.

18. For the significance of 'stories' for the forming of identity cf. Ritschl and Jones, *'Story' als Rohmaterial der Theologie*.

19. Scharfenberg and Kämpfer, *Mit Symbolen leben*, is very helpful.

20. Welker, *Gottes Geist*, 49ff.

21. Cf. sermon example 5 below: further examples of sermons in which I vary the same theme, narrative or image in cosmic, social and personal references are: 'Cain and Abel (Gen.4.1–16)', in *The Open Door*, 1–9; 'Letters to Exiles (Jer.29.1,4–14)', ibid., 24–32; 'The Sign Language of Baptism (Matt.28.18–20)', ibid., 47–51; 'On Changing Human Beings and the World (Mark 13.28–39; Luke 13.6–9)', ibid., 67–78; 'Doubting Thomas (John 20.19–29)', ibid., 117–24; 'Lichtspuren (Mt 5, 13–16)', in *Lichtspuren*, 86–92; 'Von der Sorglosigkeit der Vögel und Lilien und unseren Sorgen um sie (Mt 6, 25–34)', ibid., 93–6.

22. Cf. E.Drewermann, *Tiefenpsychologie und Exegese*, I, 484ff.

23. I am indebted to Leiner for these reflections on the rehabilitation of allegory. Cf. further Dohmen, Jacob and Söding, *Neue Formen der Schriftauslegung*.

24. For the possibility of doing pastoral work in preaching cf. C.Möller, *Seelsorglich predigen*, 69ff.

25. Cf. example 1 below, 'Simon the Tanner and Simon Peter', by Petra von Gemünden.

26. For the interpretation of the message of justification as an impulse towards cognitive restructuring cf. Theissen, *Psychological Aspects of Pauline Theology*, 252ff.

27. Cf. the brief book by the New Testament scholar H.J.Eckstein, *Erfreuliche Nachricht – traurige Hörer?*

V. Preaching as an Opportunity for Communication between Preacher and Congregation

1. Cf. Schulz von Thun, *Miteinander reden 1*; id., *Miteinander reden 2*, cf. 19–26.

2. Cf. Schulz von Thun, *Miteinander reden 2*, 38–53.

3. For 'ambiguity' as a positive quality of discourse and preaching cf. especially Engemann, *Semiotische Homiletik*, 153ff.

4. Cf. Schulz von Thun, *Miteinander reden 2*, 47.

5. As far as I know, Glebe-Moeller, *Politisk Dogmatik*, 98–103, is the first to have used the four criteria of the validity of communicative ethics for homiletics. The last chapter was prompted by him.

6. Cf. Danowski, *Kompendium der Predigtlehre*, 134–40.

7. Cf. Riemann, 'Die Persönlichkeit des Predigers'; Denecke, *Persönlich*

Predigen.

8. Cf. Denecke, *Persönlich Predigen*, esp.64–71.

9. Cf. Schulz von Thun, *Miteinander reden* 2, 61ff.

10. Ibid., 94.

11. Ibid., 118.

12. For this and the next point cf especially Daiber, *Predigt als religiöse Rede*, 210ff.

13. What Tholuck wrote in the preface to the second collection of his sermons in 1835 (in Wintzer, *Predigt*, 58–66), still applies: 'If we Germans knew in other spheres than that of the church the power exerted by the Word born directly of the Spirit before the preserved on its hearers, we would be even less content with the presentation of dead preparations. The sermon must be the action of the preacher in his study, but it must also be an action in the pulpit. When the preacher comes down he must feel the joy of a mother, the joy of a mother who has given birth to a child with God's blessing. Thus only where the sermon has been a twofold act of the preacher will it also be an act in its hearers' (63).

14. Otto, *Handlungsfelder der Praktischen Theologie*, 273, rightly contradicts the thesis that 'everyday language must be the language of faith and preaching. Obvious as the fulfilment of this demand might seem in the context of too superficial a concept of comprehensibility, it would necessarily keep from the hearers all that is more and other than the repetition of their everyday life, the repetition of prescriptions and restrictions of the kind conveyed by everyday language.'

15. The articles by Josuttis, 'Über den Predigtaufbau', 'Über den Predigtanfang', and 'Über den Predigtschluss', are basic.

16. The image of the division of 'three excursions into the wilderness' appears in the sermon on Luke 3.1–14.3 (= example 5 below). There is a division by experts in 'Cain and Abel (Gen.4.1–16)', in *The Open Door*, 1–9. The question of the three things one might want to take on a desert island forms the division of 'Preparation for the Journey into an Unknown Land. On Coming to Terms with Death', in *The Open Door*, 152–60.

17. There are fundamental comments on this in Josuttis, 'Der Prediger in der Predigt'.

18. In my view, Piper, 'Kommunikation und Kommunikationsstörungen in der Predigt', has demonstrated in a very illuminating way how unassimilated personal problems of the preacher can become irritations in preaching. 'However, if he can deal with his emotions, communicate with his "shadow" and recognize his own ambivalences, then he will also succeed in communicating with both individuals (through conversations) and groups (for example through preaching)' (242).

19. The homiletics of dialectical theology has incurred the suspicion, not without reason, of shhowing little human respect for the congregation. Cf. Thurneysen, 'Die Aufgabe der Predigt': 'The sermon is the place not for a

struggle for human understanding but for the understanding of God. The church is not a matter of one person moving towards another, but of all human beings turning their backs on everything human and moving towards God' (in Wintzer, *Predigt*, 117). 'The death of all that is human is the theme of preaching' (ibid., 118). Homileticians with a background in liberal theology were rightly disturbed by this, cf. Niebergall, 'Eine "unmenschliche Theorie"'. For that reason we should remember Barth's advice in his homiletics: 'The preacher must love his church. He may not want to be without his church. He must know: I belong with these others and want to share with them what I have received from God. Human tongues – and angelic tongues – are no use, if there is not this love' (*Homiletik*, 67).

20. Cf. Dahm, 'Hören und Verstehen'; Schreuder, 'The Silent Majority'.

21. Cf. '"Du sollst nicht ehebrechen!" Eine moralische Predigt gegen den Moralismus (2 Mos.20,14)', in *Lichtspuren*, 11–18.

22. Cf. Brox, *Falsche Verfasserangaben*.

23. Cf. Schweitzer, *The Quest of the Historical Jesus*.